Beta Humans

Travelling to the future of humanity

Written by Michael Macfarlane

i

For all humans who believe that we can do better.

CONTENTS

beta

adjective

**Used to describe something that is at the second
stage of development.**

Cambridge English Dictionary

INTRODUCTION

As I arrived at Luton Airport I stood idly at the luggage carousel waiting to discover if my suitcase had survived the drubbing of a short haul flight. Two young brothers had spent the prior three hours piercing the congeniality of the flight and testing the patience of those around them with persistent shouting and demands for attention. Their parents had been stoic in their ability to nonchalantly ignore them, much to the annoyance and distress of every other fellow passenger.

This is typical of the cynical new race to the bottom that is best demonstrated by budget flying. The resolve of passengers has been sorely tested as they have been incrementally stripped of their comforts and asked to contend with a litany of aggravators from which relief can only be attained through selfishness or by paying.

As budget airlines have turned up the pressure on their passengers, it follows as inevitable that the degrading experience of budget flying has been further denigrated by an increasing number of humans who, in the absence of the ability to pay more and for want of a kinder recourse of action, are fated to act selfishly. They do so by opting out of a simple and longstanding convention: behaving with mutual respect in the expectation that others will also do the same toward them.

But it's not entirely their fault. One could easily postulate an answer without asking the hard questions and so easily and expediently blame education or social media. But the reality is that many of the systems that have propagated within the modern world have disincentivized the collective endeavor of good behavior. And airlines are just the tip of the iceberg.

As humans we are programmed to co-exist. For over two thousand years we have packed ourselves into cities because of the opportunities and exciting diversions that come from close proximity to one another. In paleolithic prehistory we organized ourselves into tribes. The 'internal software' that organizes a typical human brain is inherently programmed toward the betterment of individuals and society through polite and congenial cooperation.

Yet this 'internal software' has now been augmented by our modern access to tools and artificial forms of higher intelligence that increasingly makes our programmed disposition for inter-human cooperation seem obsolete. We share our locations and our private data. We have surrendered much of our sovereignty as individuals. Convenience means that we unwittingly favor growing interdependence with the 'operating system' of the crowded society within which we must all exist. The promise of technology is that it will improve this 'operating system' of our society far beyond the capabilities and imagination of human brains, but in return we must increasingly surrender into it. We have de facto accepted that our evolution makes it impossible to upgrade ourselves, but that we can upgrade the world in which we exist to garner further human betterment.

The problem with this is that it is inevitable that the operating system of a technology driven society will value the cold calculus of optimal efficiency without any deference to human empathy. It will incentivize what is mathematically optimal rather than what is humanly optimal. And so, to return to the budget airlines example, we simply accept the degrading conditions because the calculus of our societal platform is that cheap prices are more important than our suffering. And so a race to the bottom ensues which leaves almost all people worse off than they would have been had they been lively to cooperating against it.

At the airport baggage carousel the herd of my fellow passengers shuffled within the crowd like penguins, none of them wishing to be left on the edges at risk of bitingly cold proximity to the two noisy children. When I spotted my black plastic suitcase, extensively cracked with one wheel missing and precariously held together by remnants of baggage labels, I broke cover to retrieve it and briskly joined the exit scrum.

With just minutes to spare before the shuttle bus to the nearby railway station was due to leave, I grabbed a reviving hot chocolate and made haste for the bus stop, hindered only by several short flights of stairs that had been unfathomably built between the airport exit and the bus stop. I reached the ticket inspector at the doors to the bus with sore legs and just moments left to spare.

"You can't come on with your coffee". I glanced for a moment at the plastic lid that was firmly affixed to my laminated paper cup, and then back into the ticket inspectors eyes, expecting that I would find signs of a dry sense of British humor which maybe in my post-flight delirium I had failed to detect.

"You can't come on with your coffee" the ticket inspector repeated, this time more sternly. "But I'm thirty-six years old, I've been capably drinking from cups for more than two decades without ever scolding anyone" I protested. "If you don't throw it away you can't come on" said the inspector, gesturing toward a nearby trash can where I reluctantly discarded the untouched hot chocolate .

The clammy uncirculated air of other people's warm breath hit me as a boarded the bus, and I shuffled to position my suitcase in the tiny aisles between the seats. The bus windows were fogged by condensation and I could only just make out the sight of the industrial estates and print works that lined the road. Finally the bus pulled up outside the airport train station where its sixty passengers, each with their own suitcase, attempted to fathom the etiquette for who should have first access to the sole elevator to the platforms. Inevitably things descended into an avoidable chaos as the crowds jostled for position and attempted to instead ascend the several flights of escalators with their suitcases, prams, children and ephemera precariously balanced, before navigating the gauntlet of the opposing crowd who had already alighted from trains in the vain hope that they might eventually reach the airport.

"When did it come to this?" I thought to myself as I brushed the sweat from my face and took a breath of the crisp cold air of the platform for trains to London. It was not so long ago that, in the cocky surety of my teens and twenties, I could arrive back from another part of the world and, like others around me, feel a smug self-satisfaction at being lucky enough to have been born into the privileged existence of Western Europe. One could be entirely nonchalant about living in an advanced nation with a strong society in which things generally worked and were always getting better.

But that is rarely the case anymore.

It's not that the United Kingdom, or indeed other nations who have derived decades of betterment from various forms of capitalism, have gone backwards. But they have been adding patches and workarounds to their operating systems whilst other nations have been dramatically leaping forward with full-blown upgrades.

The result in the United Kingdom is a society in which, increasingly, people have surrendered and sacrificed their individual sovereignty in favor of a collective interdependence with an operating system that promises to use technology to make them all better off. But that operating system is not yet fit for purpose. It neither caters to the humanity of our 'internal software' nor offers the sophisticated platform needed to enable the innovative new social and economic applications that technology promises. We make sacrifices and accept the brutally cold calculus of an operating system that drives us away from the collective endeavor of human betterment, without attaining any real benefit in return.

Rather than seeking to create a beta version of their operating system, too many Western nations have instead simply patched themselves with cheap debt, deficits and the illusion of growing prosperity and wealth that is offered by constant house price inflation. Yet this approach has left behind and locked out entire younger generations, who in the fullness of time will almost inevitably start to bring down the entire operating system by voting against this status quo. The opportunity cost of this generation invoking a regressive reversion to debunked ideas such as socialism at a time when technology has the potential to do so much to improve human life, would be immense.

And it seems painfully clear to me that something very important has been forgotten during the pursuit to keep 'patching' the current Western system. And that is our duty as humans to improve the world for future generations. To leave the planet and its nations and its societies in a better place than it was when we entered into it. To create societies and 'operating systems' that allow people to be their best and to be at their best toward one another. And to dispose of the kind of cold thinking that has seen the budget airline experience degrade us of our humanity and deprive us of our collective endeavor to grow and to thrive as humans.

This is not a new concept. The enlightenment of the 1700's represented a huge leap forward in the sophistication of human beings and the way in which our societies thought and functioned. By the start of the Victorian era in 1837 levels of inequality in Britain were a disgrace for an 'intelligent' species, but by embracing enlightenment values and philosophies and ways of thinking, by the end of Queen Victoria's reign in 1901, towns and cities had been furnished with parks and infrastructure which, in the case of London, are still the backbone of life for millions of people even today.

The opportunities currently available to humanity across technology and life sciences are so substantial as to be beyond description. And the submission of our individualism into a collective interdependence is not entirely flawed. Outsourcing our betterment to a technology driven 'world platform' gives us the space and hope to glimpse at the opportunity to affirm the purpose and human life: that our purpose as humans, as nations, as societies and as communities should be the continual betterment and improvement of how every single human experiences life on our shared planet. It's a promise that makes us feel good. But at what cost?

We should pause here to be clear that this book is not filled with the musings of someone with the power to change societies and nations. I am not an academic, an economist, a politician or even an accomplished writer. To these cliques I am an intellectual and social outsider.

I am simply an individual from an entirely unremarkable background. Someone whose Indian-born immigrant grandmother pressed upon him the need to work hard to break out from the constraints of working poverty. Someone who was proudly taken by his father to buy his first pair of molded plastic work boots before starting the first of many youthful summers working as a welders assistant. Someone who through ardent endeavor has managed to experience a life that the circumstances of its start deemed unlikely. And someone who believes that humans can do better.

Humans are now capable of betterment and advancement in ways that previous generations could not imagine. Much of that betterment will come from technology. But it will not come from inserting microchips into our brains or the bionic augmentation of our bodies. It will not come from improvement of the individual human but from upgrading our existence.

As humans we stand at a juncture between the biological limitations of the 'internal software' created during our relatively primitive beginnings, which cannot really be 'upgraded' far beyond our biological limitations, and the opportunity to substantially improve and augment human life by upgrading the thing that we can improve: the global operating system.

We can create the beta version of our world.

We can be beta humans.

HOW TO GET BETA?

To become beta humans we must first reconcile the limitations of our internal software. We are little more than the highly evolved cousins of apes using our internal software to process data and make decisions. Everything around us is just data. Every interaction, every thought and every instinct is simply the processing of data by the incomprehensibly complex network of neural connections that exist as a mass of ever-changing grey matter between our two ears.

There is nothing within our 'internal software' that creates a particular disposition for say, capitalism or socialism. That we structure nations and societies around the rules of these concepts is a function of our history and our inclination to create order. And neither is our 'operating system' constrained by the status quo. Despite the limitations of our internal software, collectively we do have the capacity to break away from what we know in pursuit of a higher truth.

The trouble is that nobody really knows what that truth is. Even those of a religious persuasion who claim to know truth can barely agree amongst themselves. So what are we to do if as a species we are to achieve the next nadir of our evolution? How can we escape the expediency of everyday life and instigate the beta version of the current operating system of our societies without a clear road map of what that should look like?

A human brain uses 20% of the power that is generated by a typical human, and so the inbuilt human survival instinct is to conserve this energy. Humans will spend most of their life in the neural equivalent of 'standby mode'. It is not within our evolution to elevate our thinking beyond our own direct experiences that have ensured our survival so far, and our 'internal software' is programmed to avoid such neurological largesse.

Yet we already know that humanity becomes greater when the majority of human beings are operating at their full neurological capacity. People who lived through the enlightenment existed alongside unimaginable deprivations in human life, yet that same period produced some of the finest art and best architecture in the history of mankind and saw huge leaps forward in human thinking and understanding. The period after World War II saw unprecedented innovations to improve human life, but it was as a function of a very dark period of destruction and death.

And so one has to ask whether the bright light of human progress can only emerge from a place of darkness? Does our 'internal software' only allow us to upgrade the world when it is coming from a place of failure, or can we leapfrog humanity from a pretty good place into a really great one without first enduring disruption?

This is important, because we all find ourselves in the Twenty First Century as the most fortunate human beings who have ever walked the planet. Our quality of life, access to food and healthcare have no prior precedent. Even overpopulation of a planet, which is by far the biggest risk to our existence far in excess of the dangers posed by climate change, has so far been mitigated by technological innovations. Extreme poverty is falling fast worldwide and the average level of comfort enjoyed by a person living in the West surpasses that of all past kings and emperors combined.

This rapid evolution of our economies and social systems has created an abundance of energy and leisure which has conspired to make it even easier for an average human brain to erode time in 'standby mode'.

And so the question becomes, how can human brains be engaged out of their 'standby mode' to create an even better world? How can Western democracies upgrade their societies to allow even more humans to do what they do best when, by any objective measure, we are already doing exceptionally well? Life is no longer a fight for survival. And the irony is that at the exact moment in our human evolution that we have the technology and freedom to elevate ourselves to places beyond all previous imagination, we also find ourselves idle in the comfort of our relative prosperity and unable to uncouple ourselves from the flawed aims that our current societal operating system wants us to focus on.

We exist at an unprecedented nexus of opportunities for the upgrade and improvement of our operating system. But to achieve this humans must first adopt bold new ideas that go far beyond the expediency of the status quo. We must collectively redefine the purpose of the relatively short time that we will spend as sentient beings. And we must remind ourselves that the opportunity of being alive happens only once in an eternity, and that what we leave behind really matters.

But we must also not lose sight of the fact that history has been a constant conflict between lofty political theories and the practical realities. One only has to look at the devastation caused by Communism to realize that the line between a noble endeavor and the dogmatic pursuit of ideology to the detriment of all human kindness and empathy, is a very fine one indeed.

So how do we get beta?

To become beta humans does not require massive social revolution or the overthrow of Governments. It does not require hordes of protestors to occupy our streets with their iPhones to document and share their virtue with their online followers. It does not require a departure from our history or from current prosperity.

Beta humans can arise through a chain reaction of compound upgrades to everything that is around us. By elevating our thinking and endeavors so that our collective life mission is to discover just how much 'upgrading' that we can implement and achieve within our countries, societies and communities within the relatively short time that we spend on the planet.

And, importantly, those upgrades need not be a step into the unknown realms of new invention. Beta humans can also arise by taking existing ideas and concepts and technologies and gradually synthesizing and upgrading them into even better ones. The world as we know it is already a colossal incubator of ideas. Cities and nations are already mastering iterative upgrades that others can easily follow and adopt. And so to upgrade our operating systems we simply need to emulate the most successful ideas, copy them, and then synthesize new ideas from them for the next iteration of upgrades. Beta humans are improvers, builders and upgraders. And the world is already full of inspiration.

BLAKE'S JERUSALEM

If the tools and opportunities to become beta humans already exist in the world, and if nations and cities are already pioneering the upgrades to the 'operating system' of their societies, then one has to ask why beta humans have not risen already? This gets to the heart of what it will take to become the first beta humans.

To create the invisible bonds of an unspoken collective endeavour to upgrade everywhere and everything to the betterment of all human beings will not be easy. But it is also not without precedent. And the best place to explore that precedent is a pub in the United Kingdom.

Over 600 pubs in the United Kingdom are named 'The Red Lion'. Historically lions were the most in vogue animal to appear within a crest of arms, and so the origins of the popular pub name most likely lies in the crests of arms of the now-forgotten landowners in the areas where more than 600 Red Lion's have endured.

The first time that I got wholly inebriated it was in a Red Lion pub in a small market town in the deprived post-industrial midlands heartland of the United Kingdom, where I grew up. It was the Euro'96 soccer tournament and England were playing Scotland. My father, a Glaswegian welder who started his first apprenticeship aged 14 and who has never taken a day off work for illness in his life, decided that he would annoy the overwhelmingly English crowd that had gathered to watch the game by continually singing 'Flower of Scotland'. For my part, with little-to-no interest in soccer, I took full advantage of the fact that the pub landlord held no qualms about serving alcohol to a 13-year-old. I can still remember the ground moving beneath my feet as I staggered home afterward.

'Flower of Scotland' is the strident and enduring national anthem of Scotland. The equivalent in Wales is 'Hen Wlad Fy Nhadau'. But England has no national anthem. Of course, for the 'United Kingdom of Great Britain and Northern Ireland' of which England, Scotland and Wales are constituent parts along with

Northern Ireland, the national anthem is 'God Save The Queen'. But England has no official national anthem.

This curious state of affairs is typical of a great many unfathomable British idiosyncrasies. When it comes to international sports England, Scotland, Northern Ireland and Wales each field their own separate teams, but at the Olympics, the United Kingdom enters a joint team known as "Team GB". The rules for Cricket are even more despairing. The international team is called 'England' but actually it is England with Wales. Until 1992 the 'England' cricket team also included Scotland and Northern Ireland, but because 'England' is a test side but Scotland and Northern Ireland aren't, players for the latter cannot qualify to play international cricket for the 'England' team. Understand? Me neither.

When I last found myself in Washington DC, I took the time to line up with the tourists escaping the scrum of the crowds of the Smithsonian and sought sanctuary in the quiet of The National Archives. The National Archives are a curious feature on the Washington tourist map. Faced with the myriad themed buildings of the Smithsonian Museum, the White House, the Lincoln Memorial and the Washington Monument, many Washington tourists will overlook the Archives.

And much like visitors to the Louvre in Paris make a beeline for the Mona Lisa – which must be amongst the most underwhelming exhibits in Paris - and international visitors to the British Museum in London head straight for the Egyptian Mummies whilst the British head for the fabulously huge scones ("biscuits" if you are an American) that are served in the Grand Atrium café, at the National Archives every visitor lines up with one intention: to view the original US Constitution and the Declaration of Independence.

After standing in line ("queuing" if you're British) patiently for some time inside the corridors of the National Archives, and going through the cold and utilitarian airport-style security checks, eventually I made it into a kind of 'holding pen' comprised from velvet barriers inside the grand marble rotunda of the National Archives. Every five minutes the imperious security guards would allow a few people to break free from the holding pen to enjoy their brief time with the US Constitution and the Declaration of Independence.

The magnitude of importance of these documents cannot be understated. They are the underpinnings of a country that set the trajectory for the world throughout the twentieth century and which remains the world's only superpower. Even as a Brit, being close to those documents in the dimmed protective lights of the rotunda was an almost spiritual experience.

The influence of the Constitution and Declaration of Independence is well-documented, but for me, as for many British people, their importance is brought most into focus by the well-told events of December 1941.

For two years before December 1941 Britain had stood alone in the world with cast iron resolve in the face of the most heavily equipped and militarized empire in all of human history. As the Nazis' crystal-meth fuelled Blitzkrieg advanced rapidly through Western Europe,

Winston Churchill declared to his fellow Britons that "If this long island history of ours is to end at last, let it end only when each of us lies choking on his own blood upon the ground". This quote pairs very well with the likely apocryphal story that in the darkest days of World War II, Churchill interrupted a family dinner in a state of melancholy to make his wife and children promise that, if the Nazis invaded Britain, each would do their duty when faced with probable death by making sure to "take one of them with you".

And as I had stood under the Rotunda inside The National Archives, I couldn't help but reflect on the fact that there was no equivalent grand rotunda for me to visit in Great Britain. Despite all of the similarities in values between the United States and Great Britain, at least in reference to Twentieth century events, the latter does not have a Constitution. Except it does. It's just that nobody has ever actually written it down.

How ineffably British is that? That the entire 'playbook' for the building of a nation was based on a constitution that existed only in the sound application of the principles and precedents that exist in the collective documents and imagination and memories of its people.

"But Magna Carta is the British constitution!" I hear you declare? Well it is. And it isn't. The Magna Carta may have laid the foundation for everything that followed by placing the law above the kings own will, which was a revolutionary idea in 1215. And it also prescribed some rights such as the right of "free men" to a trial by jury. But there are three things that strike you when you visit one of the four surviving original copies of Magna Carta, as I did one recent summers day when I visited Salisbury Cathedral, which is home to the best-preserved copy of the original Magna Carta.

The first is the magnificent beauty of the thirteenth century Chapter House within Salisbury Cathedral where the Magna Carta is displayed. On a bright day the Chapter House seems almost unreal in its beauty. The light charges through the stained glass windows and illuminates a room of such magnificence that it captivates all of the senses. And that is the first problem. Because I was so taken by the location, that the Magna Carta itself – kept in a dark booth in the centre of the room - seemed a little stale by comparison.

The second problem is something that I and many English-speaking tourists before me have often and foolishly failed to anticipate before seeing Magna Carta. That the entire document is written in abbreviated medieval Latin. You can, as I did, press your nose firmly up against the protective glass case to get a closer look at the text, but unless you dedicated your early schooling to the study of Latin, and unless you can recall anything beyond remembering to *semper ubi sub ubi*, then don't expect to garner any enlightenment by reading the original Magna Carta.

The third problem is that the notion of Magna Carta and its protection of ancient personal liberties is a constitutional fiction and a persistent political myth. In truth, the majority of Magna Carta is given over to the relatively trivial matters of the time when it was written; and the overwhelming majority of it has subsequently been repealed in the years hence. Furthermore, Magna Carta provides no check-in-principle to Parliament legislating against the rights of citizens. All that is needed is an act of Parliament, and individuals can be held without trial and refused a lawyer. This would be undeniably unconstitutional in the USA. But not in Britain under Magna Carta.

And yet despite this lack of a written constitution, Great Britain has been the most stable country in the world since 1066. It is a country of relative prosperity and freedom. British voters show disdain for revolutionary ideas, and the British sense of humor means that no 'strong man' leader can prevail over democracy because when presented with 'revolutionary' ideas the British will, to use common parlance, "take the piss."

But despite all of this, England does not even have its own national anthem. Sure England is the foundation of Great Britain, and Great Britain has 'God Save the Queen'. But the reality is that when impassioned to express national pride, there is only one anthem that the English will sing. Its position is entirely unofficial yet it is wholeheartedly adopted. It's called 'Jerusalem'.

This strident and vivid anthem long ago won the hearts of the English: a survey conducted by the BBC in 2006 showed that fifty-five percent of the English thought it should be the nation's official anthem. The hymn started life as a poem by William Blake in the preface of his epic 'Milton: A Poem In Two Books' which was first printed in 1808. And more than a century later the composer Sir Hubert Parry added the music, in 1916.

The hymn implies that a visit by Jesus would create heaven in England, inspired by the story that a young Jesus travelled to England during his unknown years. The theme is linked to the Book of Revelations (3:12 and 21:2) which describes a Second Coming, wherein Jesus establishes a 'new Jerusalem'. A quick Google search will bring up the four stanzas of lyrics, but the final stanza is perhaps the most illuminating:

I will not cease from mental fight;
Not shall my sword sleep in my hand
Till we have built Jerusalem
In England's green and pleasant land.

'Jerusalem' is a loosely veiled declaration that no matter what the English are faced with, no matter how hard life becomes, that together, they will build their own version of Heaven – their own 'Jerusalem' - in "England's green and pleasant land".

This matters a lot for beta humans.

For more than a century 'Jerusalem' was a manifestation of the invisible bonds of collective endeavour in the UK. And beta humans can similarly only rise when the minds of individuals are provoked out of 'standby mode' and similarly roused into an unspoken collective endeavour to upgrade all of our 'operating systems'. It must be a libertarian endeavour achieved without authoritarian coercion or 'nudging' by the armies of behaviour psychologists now employed by Governments. It can only be achieved when individuals exert their sovereign influence as consumers and voters. Beta humans do not need an anthem to achieve this. But they do need a credible and convincing way to instil confidence in the invisible bonds that will bind people into the collective endeavour of improving and upgrading everything to achieve levels of human betterment beyond what can be attained as individuals. People from all walks of life must be convinced that if they commit themselves to upgrading the 'operating system' of their country, society and community, then others will also be equally selfless in their commitment to the same endeavour.

Incidentally, the United States has its own, perhaps more explicit, version of 'Jerusalem' in the rally call that the United States is "the greatest country on Earth" - despite an avalanche of objective evidence to the contrary. At the time of writing The United States ranks 29th in the world for education, has a healthcare system that ranks 37th in the world for efficiency, and is the fattest nation in history. But to use this objective evidence is to completely misunderstand the "greatest country" rallying call, because it has never mattered whether the USA was objectively "the greatest". Much like 'Jerusalem' it was simply a national 'mission statement' that bound all Americans into the endeavour.

The example of twentieth century Britain and the Unites States provides a template for the collective endeavour that must be achieved before beta humans can start to upgrade and improve everything. But to find inspiring examples of how to upgrade the operating systems of society, beta humans must start to look to other parts of the world that are rapidly 'upgrading'.

THE UNITED STATES OF AMERICA

The USA is unique in the world. A huge cluster of fifty states, each representing a laboratory for the testing of products and systems and ideas and concepts. A success in one state can be quickly and easily duplicated into the forty nine other states and then scaled into a national platform for taking on the world. No other country in the world can even come close to boasting such a successful platform for nation-building.

This has established the United States as the greatest "empire of the mind" in all of human history, a great force for good ever since Great Britain passed on the gilded baton of empire. In 1939 all of Britain's gold was transferred to the USA to pay for the war as part of Operation Fish, and at that moment Britain effectively ceded global supremacy to the USA - as well as the responsibility to police and occasionally save the world.

But now the titanic supremacy of this twentieth century superpower is facing a challenge with near equivalence to Operation Fish that could irrevocably diminish its stature. China now holds over $1 trillion in American debt and so could, in theory, hold the US economy to ransom with the threat of selling these vast US treasury holdings. Such an action would be an ironic repetition of the 1956 threat by the USA to sell its vast holdings of British bonds during the Suez crisis if Britain did not accept that it was no longer a global power and back down (which Britain duly did – marking the final end of Britain's status as a global empire and superpower).

In 1970 an American 30-year-old had a ninety per cent chance of earning more than their parents earned at the same age, once adjusted for inflation. By 1980 a 30-year-old still had an eighty per cent chance of making more money than their parents. But by 2016 about half of 30-year-olds were earning less than their parents were at the same age. And that worrying trend also holds when comparing 40-year-olds to their parents.

Whilst on the whole the average US worker's income has increased by 77% since 1970 once adjusted for inflation, wages for the households in the bottom half of earners have seen no rise in real income at all since the 1970's. Instead, almost all of the income gains have gone to those at the very top, with incomes for the top one per cent rising by an astonishing 216% during the period. This change in distribution of US income and substantial loss of social mobility represents the fraying of the collective endeavour of the "American Dream". As inequality rises, trust levels and educational outcomes also decline, and politics becomes more polarised too. This creates a vicious cycle of deadlock that renders Governments incapable of addressing what is causing the problem, and the USA now seems more politically divided than at any time in living memory at the very moment that geopolitical forces are uncertain.

But could beta humans rescue the United States by filling the void left by the absconditure of the American Dream with the beta human endeavour to upgrade the country's operating systems? Could beta humans unlock the potential of every human and end the current division in the United States by eliminating inequality, reinstating social mobility and uniting the nation in a fresh collective purpose and meaning? This notion is in fact already being tested in a trinity of US cities that are together incubating an alternative future that places technology at the heart of human betterment.

These three cities wield such a huge cultural, technological and economic influence on the trajectory of the entirety of humanity that, at least to an outsider, they challenge the notion of "one nation, indivisible". It's a West Coast trinity of cities that are collectively reimagining and reshaping the world, and exporting their technologies and philosophies and influence. Their collective promise is not of the 'American Dream', but of building a better world that is outside of the scope of current human imagination. They are collectively a de facto 'nation of the mind' rather than one of geography. And they could become the crucible from which the very first beta humans will emerge.

The cities in question are Seattle, Los Angeles and San Francisco - and their surrounding metropolitan areas.

The list of twenty first century entrepreneurs, innovators and companies from these cities who have disrupted and reinvented and influenced the world is huge. Seattle is home to Amazon, Boeing, Starbucks and Microsoft. San Francisco has given the world Google, Facebook, AirBnb, Uber, YouTube, eBay, Apple and Twitter. And for several decades the movie and television and music studios of LA have consistently set the tone for the world's popular culture.

For many the sound of their early teens comes from a popular musician or band. But for me it was the sound of a modem attempting to make a dial-up Internet connection. In those days the Internet was a strange and barren place. It was occupied mostly by conspiracy theorists who could for the first time compare stories and share blurry photos that 'proved' the existence of Government cover-ups about aliens and UFOs. The only online social activity was in the AOL chat rooms. Websites had to be found using a portal service such as Yahoo because the first functioning search engine called AltaVista was like a flickering candle in a dark room until Google came along and lit up the Internet just a few years later. Amazon had already opened the world's most prominent online store selling books, but they were only available to buy in the USA. The early Internet heralded a new age and spurred on awkward teens like me to experiment and enterprise with new innovations. Today many believe that the streets of Silicon Valley are paved with the technological gold derived from the subscription of technology entrepreneurs to the creed of finding new applications of Internet-enabled technologies that are adopted so quickly they grow exponentially and create spectacular wealth – often without even having to make a profit.

I arrived in San Francisco during Columbus Day weekend, which also coincided with Fleet Week: a Navy, Marine Corps and Coast Guard tradition in which active military ships dock in a variety of major cities for one week. The tradition started in 1935, when ships would dock and locals would take in sailors for home visits, but its incarnation as a huge San Francisco event attracting over one million visitors to a city with a resident population of just 870,800 started in 1981.

The main highlights of Fleet Week are the Air Show on San Francisco Bay, with performances by the Blue Angel stunt planes; and also a parade of ships under the Golden Gate Bridge. I had arrived in the city without any knowledge of my fortuitous timing, though I should have realized when I couldn't find a single hotel room that was reasonably priced. I ended up booking what promoted itself as an elegant 1920's neo-gothic hotel with a self-proclaimed "Film-Noire-style" in an area called the 'Tenderloin'. That was a big mistake.

The hotel didn't seem to have been refurbished or decorated since at least 1970, and inside it looked like it hadn't been properly cleaned in decades. The paint was peeling from the walls, the carpets were thick with human detritus, the bathroom suite was black with rot, wires emanated from the blood-stained skirting boards and I was woken every morning to the sound of an extremely overweight couple having very loud sex against the paper-thin walls. The reasons that I know that they were overweight do not bare description.

Over the course of my stay, complaining to the nonchalant receptionist-come-concierge became a daily occurrence. Each day, usually after waiting for a long time for her to finish a personal phone call or a conversation with a colleague, I would get the same reply from her in response to my increasing state of despair: "I'm sorry Sir, but it's an old hotel, nearly one hundred years, so there's really nothing that we can do about it". I wanted to respond that a great many of my fellow countrymen live in houses that are over one hundred years old, but whilst that may be a reason that a building develops more problems than a modern one, it is certainly not an excuse for dilapidation And what is more, one hundred years is not "old", and by British standards is positively modern for a formerly grand hotel: Brown's Hotel in London opened in 1837 and remains today as clean and seductively opulent as the very day that it opened. So rather than telling me that the hotel is poor because of its age, how about just being honest and admitting that the hotel is managed by an ambush of lazy and incompetent employees who were eluded of all talents except for the having the savvy to massively jack up the prices for unsuspecting guests during the busiest week of the year?

But instead I said nothing.

The second reason that my choice of hotel was a mistake was its location in the Tenderloin. Whilst the rest of San Francisco has got fancier and more expensive, the Tenderloin hasn't just remained resistant to gentrification, but has travelled in the opposite direction. During the Gold Rush of 1848-1855, the Tenderloin was the spot to spend your money at brothels, restaurants, theatres and hotels; and for decades visitors kept flocking to its speakeasies, jazz clubs and gambling parlours. By the 1950's this made the Tenderloin one of San Francisco's most prosperous neighbourhoods. But today the Tenderloin looks like a real-life set for television series The Walking Dead. Hundreds of mentally ill, degenerate and drug-addled homeless spend their days in giant street communities. Many of them seem to who have completely lost themselves for whatever reason and have had their humanity so purloined by narcotics that they show very little awareness that they even exist within a reality.

2014 US Department of Housing data suggests that San Francisco is second only to New York for the number of homeless people per square mile, with 149 compared to New York's 211. But in New York more homeless people get sheltered, which means that the homelessness in San Francisco is more visually pervasive. I would go as far as to say that it is worse and uglier in San Francisco than anywhere else in the USA, and so much so that it is dangerously close to becoming a "famous" attribute of the city. You can't help but wonder how a city at the crucible of the life-enhancing innovations and technologies that define liberal capitalism as an engine for human progress, can also be home to some of Americas most visible extremes of human deprivation? How can the home of companies that consistently define the basis of their very profitable existence as being part of a mission to improve humanity, exist cheek-to-cheek with such a visible community of people who have been so completely and hopelessly left behind, and not undertake to solve the problem?

This is a challenge that beta humans must solve. History teaches us that when a powerful global empire embraces rapid technological and economic progress, it is often accompanied by great chasms of inequality. And if the 'empire of the mind' of the US 'technology trinity' is not improving the operating system of the humans within even its local community, then the promise of that technology cannot then be deployed to drive human betterment by upgrading the wider world.

This notion of an American 'empire of the mind' is a repeating one. American history teaches that empires are geographic and tyrannical, and that the Declaration of Independence grew directly out of rebellion against empire. And so it is unpalatable for most Americans to consider themselves at the head of an inescapably influential global empire. American citizens see no overseas colonies, no imperialism, no tyranny – and so they do not see their empire, even whilst they enjoy the fruits of it: the USA represents 4.4% of the global population but was responsible for 23% of global GDP in 2018. The only precedent for this is the British Empire, with 2.5% of the global population enjoying 24% of the global GDP at the Empires' 1870 zenith.

The truth is that the technology titans of West Coast American are modern-day incarnations of the East India Company that expanded the domains of the British Empire. They are economic imperialists who extend their cultural and economic influence across the planet, capturing an ever-greater share of economic activity and exporting the value back to their shareholders in the United States, whilst putting very little back into other countries, where they make a negligible tax contribution. Much like the British empire claimed it was bringing commerce and democracy, the tech imperialists claim to be bringing "progress". It's an unpalatable proposition that risks undermining the very promise of technology that would give rise to a new enlightenment and the world's very first beta humans.

The East India company was a British joint-stock company owned by elite merchants and aristocrats - the 1% of their day - that was formed to trade with the East Indies and later expanded across China and gained monopoly control of large parts of the Indian subcontinent. By 1803 the Company had a private army of 260,000 - twice that of the British Army – and had risen to account for a large proportion of British trade. It even issued its own money. The Company traded mainly in commodities that were exotic to Britain such as cotton, salt, silk, opium and tea. A single-minded focus on establishing trade monopolies throughout Asia made the Company the heralding agents of the British Imperial Empire, despite operating as an independent company that was deliberately far-removed from any direct control by the British Crown. The East India Company became the darling of the London Stock Market, which it dominated for most of the Eighteenth Century whilst it extended its dominions across the subcontinent and transferred great swathes of capital back to Britain to deepen the capital markets. The Company's entrepreneurial energy spurred British prosperity through a culture of trade and adventurism.

It is very hard to describe the East India Company without fireworks of brain activity drawing obvious comparisons to the global tech titans of West Coast America. At the time of writing the market capitalisation of Apple is greater than the GDP of countries such as Turkey, Saudi Arabia and The Netherlands. A quarter of the world's population – 1.94 billion – are active users of Facebook. Amazon owns more than 90% market share across 5 different product popular categories and is quickly growing toward an effective monopoly not just in ecommerce, but in global retail. Starbucks has nearly thirty thousand stores in over fifty countries. Boeing enjoys a 43% global market share in aviation. Uber has 75 million users across the world. AirBnB is completely disrupting the long-established global hotel and hospitality industry. And much like the East India

Company issued its own currency that was independent of sovereign nations, blockchain technology means that the entrepreneurs of Silicon Valley are issuing new cryptocurrencies that will challenge the sovereign monopoly of Governments over monetary policy.

These US commercial titans are undoubtedly the agents of a massive global empire. It is not an empire based on territories or outposts – though one could argue that every international Starbucks is like a mini-satellite of the motherland – but an empire of the mind derived from colossal cultural and technological power and commercial might. America does not need territories to validate or prove its position in the world: it has redefined global empire. Forcing this point, and somewhat ironically, the flag of the East India Company is considered to have inspired the Grand Union Flag of the USA. To look at the flag of the Company is to see the star-spangled banner of the United States, but with the fifty stars replaced by the indelible Union Jack flag of Great Britain. Benjamin Franklin once gave a speech to George Washington that endorsed adopting the Company's flag as the national flag of the United States, and some colonists felt that the Company could be a powerful ally in the War of Independence, and so they also flew it too.

Muck like the East India company, most of these agent-of-empire tech companies extract huge economic and commercial value from the countries where they operate without giving much back in return. In 2016 Amazon had sales of £19.5 billion in Europe but booked its sales through Luxembourg so that its corporation tax bill was just £7.4m. Between its launch in 1998 and 2012 Starbucks paid just £8.4m in corporation tax in the UK despite £3 billion of revenues. In 2017 Google paid £36 million in UK tax despite UK revenues in excess of £1 billion.

This all underlines the problem with empires built by commercial agents, and the huge problem facing beta humans. Commercial agents may start with good intentions to change the world, but they get increasingly drawn and distracted by the huge profits and wealth that is on offer. When Google listed on the Stock Exchange in 2014, it's manifesto included the maxim "Don't be evil". By 2018 the motto had been quietly dropped.

And so at the exact moment in history that the USA is facing a crisis of confidence in the American Dream, it must also deal with the collective hubris of titanic companies whose global influence has grown to potentially dangerous proportions. The East India Company ended when, tired of being economically subjugated, the populace of its Indian territories rebelled, precipitating a violent and murderous retaliation by the Company that gave the British Government cause to effectively abolish it in 1858. Could the technology titans of the West Coast face a similarly abrupt end when their global user bases tire of the heralding agent tech companies disrupting their local industries and extracting huge value from their local communities without putting anything back in?

The big question for beta humans is whether the West Coast titans will be able to pivot to avoid this fate, and instead harness their powers to usher in the age of beta humans. Or will they continue to move away from the maxim of "don't be evil" in the relentless pursuit of commercial gain? To a large extent, what these companies choose to do next, and how they choose to interact with their local communities and global dominions, will very likely determine how soon that the world might see its first beta humans. If the technology titans do not change, the dawn of the age of the beta humans could still be decades or even centuries away.

I thought about this more whilst watching the Blue Angels perform in the skies above San Francisco. In most countries an air show might last for a couple of hours, but such is the proliferate military spending of the USA that they seemingly performed throughout the day as a permanent fixture in the sky. Each time that my gaze got used to the aerial acrobatics and my attention started to wander back to the unique architecture of the city, one or more of the airplanes would unleash an after-burner and the roaring sound of the jet engine would demand the attention of everyone in the city who stopped to look up. It was spectacular.

The one problem with this is that walking the streets required more attention than usual, because they were teeming with people preparing to take part in the Columbus Day parade. Everywhere there were people dressed up and putting the finishing touches to decorated cars and parade floats that must have taken huge efforts to create. The atmosphere was one of busy excitement, and as the sun shone, it was hard not to reflect on the sense of cohesion and unity.

There was another reason that I had such warm feelings of happy contentment whilst walking the streets of San Francisco, and it's something that I will call the 'Hampstead effect'. Hampstead is an area a few miles North of central London that is known for its intellectual, literary and artistic connections and for a large expanse of hilly parkland known as Hampstead Heath. It is also the most expensive part of London, with more millionaires than any other area in Britain.

Hampstead became a spa town in the 18th Century when many grand houses were built, and by the 19th Century a new railway connection to central London made it a popular suburb and something of a playground for affluent Londoners. But the Hampstead of today really started to take shape in 1906 when redoubtable activist and social reformer Henrietta Barnett set up the Hampstead Garden Suburb Trust and purchased 243 acres of land that had been owned by the prestigious Eton College. Barnett appointed Raymond Unwin as architect to design a new housing scheme that would be based on six principles that she had devised: That it should cater for all classes of people and all income groups. That there should only be low housing density. That roads should be wide and tree lined. That gardens should be separated by hedges, not walls. That local woods and public gardens should be free to all. And that it should be quiet, with no church bells. When Unwin pointed out that some of Barnett's request would infringe local bylaws, Henrietta persuaded the Government to pass an Act of Parliament to allow it.

The result was Hampstead Garden Subhurb, a triumph of town planning for the middle classes of handsome houses spaced along wide tree-lined boulevards clustered around wide open public spaces. Men could commute to their jobs as mid-level bank clerks and insurance salesmen in central London whilst their wives looked after their perfectly harmonious and beautiful family accommodation and their children attended the local schools. It was a community designed and built to bring harmony to the soul. And, perhaps most importantly, it was an idealised way of living that was entirely within the reach of the middle classes.

Henrietta Barnett had successfully redefined a new standard for all future developments: drawing from her Christian Socialist beliefs she had cast a new precedent from which all future town planning and semi-urban development could take a cue to build the kind of homes and communities that families deserved. No doubt in her mind, her fine example would lead to a future where high-quality housing set within harmonious communities would be in plentiful supply to families in all income groups, who would refuse to settle for anything less. She must have reasonably believed that it would 'change the game', and in 1917 Barnett was named a Commander of the Order of the British Empire in recognition of her achievement.

Unfortunately Britain did not have a plentiful supply of women as redoubtable as Henrietta Barnett, and rather than become the rule, Hampstead still stands out today as the exception. As London grew the wealthy fled outward to Hampstead's pristine streets, pushing up prices and turning a place that had been conceived as a place for typical everyday families people into one for only the super-exclusive and very wealthy elite. Today a stroll around Hampstead is extremely pleasant, and it serves as a model for the kind of lifestyle - in architectural and town planning terms - that should be available to all. It is a sharp contrast to the high rise 'communist-architecture-but-with-balconies' that is sprouting up all over London and parts of Britain. But it's a great shame that it now requires wealth to be able to live in a community that is designed to set the standard of what 'normal living' would and should look like for everyday people in Britain.

And that is the feeling that one also gets in San Francisco, where the median house price has climbed from just over $600k in 2012 to over $1.6 million in 2018. The unique and idiosyncratic houses, the steep streets, the view of the bay, the bars, the coffee houses, the coastal walks and hidden beaches that are West of the Golden Gate Bridge – all of it represents a model template for an everyday life as part of a local community that should be accessible to everyone, but which in modern times has instead become a preserve of the elite. And that is another big problem for the prospect of beta humans emerging from the West Coast. Because the wider benefits of technological progress for everyday people living nearby are being 'crowded out' - to use an economics term - by the accelerated prosperity of the very architects of that progress. The benefits of technology, such as mildly cheaper taxis that can be hailed more efficiently, shopping delivered to your door, the ability to buy and sell online or sharing photos with friends and family: it all starts to feel superficial when an average young person cannot realistically afford to buy a decent house in a nice community where they can start a family.

San Francisco is of course a spectacular city. After strolling Pier 39 to see the sea lions, visiting the Ghirardeli Chocolate Factory, drinking cocktails at Fort Mason, hiking the coastal path from the Golden Gate Bridge and generally taking in the beautiful streets, I resolved that I wouldn't be able to complete my trip without making the first-time-tourist pilgrimage to Alcatraz Island, which was America's most notorious prison between 1934 and 1963. The most famous inmate at Alcatraz was Al Capone, who arrived in 1934 and stayed for four and a half years. Two years earlier the federal authorities had cleverly and successfully prosecuted him for tax evasion when they were unable to make a good criminal case against him for the St Valentine's Day Massacre. Neither were they able to construct a water tight criminal case based on Capone's vast, murderous and audacious empire of illicit activities that was said to be worth the equivalent of over $62 million.

Choosing to pursue and prosecute Capone for tax evasion – rather than murder - is the kind of ingenious lateral thinking that is sadly missing in most government departments today. The most memorable example of lateral thinking in Britain occurred back in 1973, when the Greater London Council (GLC) published the Greater London Development Plan, which astonishingly proposed to demolish over two-thirds of Covent Garden, including the famous market and its neo-classical architecture, as well as the large-scale demolition of the majority of the Eighteenth and Nineteenth Century buildings around the historic old market, many of them extremely handsome buildings of great architectural and historic merit. George Gardiner, a Conservative Member of Parliament, described the new scheme to replace 96 handsome acres with a high density scheme of brutalist concrete architecture as "London's biggest and most exciting redevelopment project since the Great Fire of 1666". But if you search for images of 'The Barbican, London', you will get a good idea of what was considered "exciting" and "modern" architecture in 1970's London.

A small grassroots movement of resistance was formed, but in 1972 the disputed plans were upheld by an independent inquiry reporting to the Secretary of State for the Environment, Geoffrey Rippon. This gave Rippon a conundrum. It was not within the gift of a Minister to overturn the findings of an independent inquiry, especially when so many of the prospective developers who were attached to the new scheme were politically connected. But equally, the post-war consensus of "modernising" cities like London with the bulldozer approach to redevelopment was starting to fall apart. So Rippon did something that really should be more preeminent in modern political folklore. He approved the scheme in its entirety. And on the very same day he added 250 buildings in Covent Garden to the national register of buildings that are protected from demolition because of their historical or architectural merit. The latter made the comprehensive redevelopment of the area completely unworkable, and so despite getting their plans approved by a Secretary of State, the developers were left with no choice but to abandon their plans entirely. How I wish that modern politics gave us more stories like this.

Alcatraz is a fascinating place and home to lots of factoids and stories. The showers for example were always kept blisteringly hot so that the inmates couldn't get used to cold water and so were less likely to attempt an escape that would involve swimming 1.25 miles across the freezing waters of San Francisco bay. And the number of prisoners held was actually quite small: the prison had a capacity of just 312 and held only 1,576 prisoners in total during its thirty-year lifetime as a notorious Federal facility. But for me the greater fascination grew entirely from one place: a 1996 Michael Bay film starring Sean Connery and Nicholas Cage called 'The Rock'. It was the first DVD that I ever bought at around the age of fifteen – so early in the life of DVDs that half way through the film you had to eject the disc and turn it over to be able to continue watching. And it was the first movie that I had watched after plugging in a new speaker system and sub-woofer to my Packard Bell computer and discovering new heights of audio experience. The film was panned by critics but was a popular box office success, grossing $335 million against a production budget of $75 million. The plot is based loosely around a geeky FBI chemist (Cage) and a former SAS Captain (Connery) being tasked with stopping a rogue troop of Marines who have seized Alcatraz Island, taken hostages, and threatened to launch rockets filled with nerve gas into San Francisco unless they are paid $100 million.

But for my younger brother and I in our early teens, the basis of the plot and even the box office takings meant nothing. The film had Sean Connery. It had gratuitous violence. It had an immense car chase in a Ferrari. It had multiple explosions. It had gore. It had guns and military hardware. It had a pigtailed Vanessa Marcil engaged in flagrante delicto on a rooftop. It had everything. So I was keen to link the scenes that I had watched hundreds of times with the reality of Alcatraz. I arrived on the island and disembarked the ferry to take in the exceptional views back toward San Francisco. I stood through a barely-audible orientation, grabbed a map and headed to discover the locations that were so familiar to me in film. When 'The Rock' Director Michael Bay first saw the peeling paint and crumbling texture of Alcatraz, he decided that they were vital to the feel of the piece, so he had resisted the Studios' preference for making the movie in a studio – which would be the most economical way to make a movie – and had used the actual island. But unfortunately the nature of movie-making means it is hard to reconcile key scenes with locations. A single scene might seamlessly cut between the real Alcatraz and a studio, or suggest parts of a location link together in ways that they do not in real life; and so my search to reconcile my visit with the movie returned only echoes and shadows. Without the drama and cinematography of the movie, I didn't really get the full 'fix' that I had been hoping for, so later that night I indulged a tickling curiosity and fired up the Internet to find out how much of The Rock was actually filmed on the island. A lot of it was, however, I was also a little disappointed to discover that many of my most favourite scenes – including that rooftop scene with Vanessa Marcil - were actually filmed in studios in Los Angeles.

This highlights yet another important aspect of the 'empire of the mind' of the USA that could help to determine when the world welcomes its first beta humans. That the entertainment industry has for decades embellished, accentuated and magnified the values and image of America by using the magic of cinema to cultivate an image that is a few degrees of separation away from reality, but which resonates with the American people and which – either by design or by happy coincidence – heightens perceptions of the USA and its values amongst billions of people worldwide.

This colossal soft power is a core tenet of the American Empire. Whereas the British Empire relied on the maxim gun, the American Empire uses Hollywood and McDonalds to exert a tremendous global influence. It says a lot that totalitarian leaders have long been envious of Hollywood's extraordinary ability to tell stories that speak to the entire planet. In what is most likely an apocryphal tale, Stalin is said to have postulated that "If I could control the medium of the American motion picture, I would need nothing else to convert the entire world to communism". And as people's preferences have become more sophisticated and their range of choices widens, this influence is extending into new arenas such as video games too.

Such is the imprint of the 'American way' onto the world's psyche that even when other countries invent something, to make it successful, they have to first make it more 'American'. The Transformers movie franchise for example is based on a Japanese toy. One of the films was filmed in China and partially financed by the Chinese. Yet the film depicts the Chinese as helpless bystanders as a group of Americans led by Mark Wahlberg 'save the day' on their own soil. Or take for example Grand Theft Auto, one of the world's most popular video games. It was conceived, designed and programmed entirely in Britain in Edinburgh, but players play the game in fictional cities that are distinctly American. This is not a case of an Edinburgh company designing the game to look and feel American because the USA represented a huge market. It is because "American" is a also global visual language.

The reason that this matters for prospective beta humans is because stories are how we all learn. The dawn of the beta humans will be marked by an unspoken and unwritten collective mission to upgrade the operating systems of the world in which all humans exist for the betterment of every human being - with none left behind. This can only manifest itself in the invisible bonds that must exist between all people who must themselves refrain from acting selfishly in order to make sure that the entirety of society are better off. And it will be whoever tells the best stories that gets to set the direction of travel into this brave new world.

The invisible bonds and connections that will lead to a new beta human era of collective human enlightenment will be borne from synthesising new behaviours from stories and experiences and interactions. And it is Hollywood who feeds this to the world and wields the power to provoke human brains out of standby mode. Hollywood even goes so far as to sugar the pill of the harder human endeavours and experiences to make them more palatable to the complicated human brain: the world presented in film and television and video games is rarely grounded in reality, but is instead packaged in a way that it is appealing to connect with. Making these connections influences the behaviours and decisions of many humans regardless of geography.

Of course, Hollywood is not overseen by totalitarian leaders or Communist propaganda ministers. Hollywood filmmakers do not, as far as we know, take calls from the White House asking them to turn a particular story into a television series or a film because they would like to shape and influence society in a particular direction. Hollywood instead looks at society and mirrors what it sees directly back at it, except with more beautiful people and happier endings – and with

America always coming out on top, often to the chagrin of those who favour the rigours of historical accuracy!

Society does not have self-configuring modular extra-terrestrial lifeforms (Transformers) or playboy ingenious superhero scientists (Iron Man) or a diminutive humanoid race inhabiting the lands of Middle-earth (Lord Of The Rings) or 'world-killer' asteroids that get defeated by regular blue-collar oil rig workers before it can exterminate humanity (Armageddon). But that is the beauty of film. Film communicates complexity and nuance in a way that our brains are naturally attuned to pick up, and so we understand much more than what we are seeing on the surface. And because of this, its influence is colossal.

Chinese academics for example, have quietly noted that the strong message of 'individualism' in Transformers has seeped through into the conformist Chinese culture. Originally Iron Man was a vehicle for its creator Stan Lee to explore Cold War themes, particularly the role of American technology and industry in the fight against communism. Lord of The Rings is a classic tale of good people coming together to defeat evil. And Armageddon…well the story is clearly about the latent potential within ordinary people to do extraordinary things, but the ageing film now has a more practical purpose as part of NASA's training programme, with staff challenged to identify the 168 occurrences in the film that are completely impossible in physics.

American novelist and satirist Kurt Vonnegut called attention to how the internal software of a human is programmed to be highly receptive to stories that have a particular 'shape'. In his Master's thesis in Anthropology for the University of Chicago, which according to Vonnegut was "rejected because it was so simple and looked like too much fun", stories have shapes that can be drawn on graph paper, and the shape of a given society's stories are at least as interesting as the shape of its pots or spearheads. Vonnegut identified eight core 'shapes' of stories that he gave mischievous names to, such as 'Man in Hole', 'Boy Meets Girl' and 'Cinderella', and through his playful analysis,

Vonnegut showed that at their core, most movies are playing back the same shapes of story again and again to program our internal software with set behaviours.

To travel from San Francisco to Los Angeles I had to engage with the only thing that I have ever seen defeat the optimistic American spirit: US domestic flights. I do not know how or when domestic flying got so bad in America, but without exception the security staff are nonchalantly condescending, the seating is grubby, the gate staff bark orders and treat passengers like unthinking cattle and the airports themselves are designed for a time that has very long since passed.

Los Angeles is another one of those American cities where the scale is vast. Europeans tend to like American cities like San Francisco because you can feasibly traverse it on foot if you have the time, but that is simply not the case in LA, where the distances are huge and the pedestrian footpaths non-existent. If you did try to walk somewhere, the exposure to exhaust fumes from the huge and congested roads would be hideous. In some ways this is a great leveller. LA is one of those cities where the amount of pleasure and enjoyment available directly equates to your level of wealth. But even if you live in a mega-mansion in the Hollywood Hills, if you want to actually go anywhere, you've got to sit in the endless traffic jams that asphyxiate the city, just like everyone else.

It is a common stereotype that almost everyone working in hospitality in LA is an aspiring actor or actress. Well I can't vouch for that, except to say that the pert and pouting receptionist at my hotel changed from Hyde into Jekyll when she learned that I was arriving with a camera crew in tow, and preceded to tell me about all of the casting couches that she had graced in recent years in her efforts to become an actress. For a moment I thought that she might be talking in euphemisms, but her serious face showed no hint or humour or irony - in fact it showed no emotional range whatsoever because of too much botox - and I suspect that her commitment to being resolutely interested in nothing except herself was the reason that she wasn't a working actress.

After spending some time making a pilgrimage to the Griffith Observatory in the Hollywood Hills to take in the exceptional views; working my way around Beverley Hills and exploring the beaches of Santa Monica and Venice, I spent the evening drinking a few too many margarita cocktails in an absolutely fantastic Mexican restaurant before accidentally staggering into a noisy bar that was full of ever-so-slightly too beautiful people. I made a swift evacuation and caught an Uber back to my hotel, where I passed out on my bed for what felt like seconds before my alarm sounded to wake me for a day of filming in South Gate.

The most frequently paraphrased statement of Karl Marx is that "religion is the opium of the people". Then at some point in recent history someone unknown posited that in fact "soccer is the opium of the masses". Actually they said "football" rather than "soccer", but when in LA it is polite to defer to the local lexicon and not be too pedantic about these things. Happily my day was going to be defined by both soccer and by religion, though I didn't know it yet as I arrived after spending nearly two hours fighting through the stationary LA traffic to travel the few miles out toward South Gate.

The vastness of LA is comprised of scores of neighbourhoods, which is why some refer to it as "forty suburbs in search of a city". The wealthy suburbs in the west side of LA are the safest: Santa Monica, Brentwood and Beverly Hills. And predictably, the poor suburbs in south LA are the ones that the Internet labels as "too dangerous to visit". South Gate might not top the list of "no go" neighbourhoods, but it apparently ranks in the top five. It is a notable suburb partly because nearly ninety five per cent of its population of 94,000 identify as Hispanic or Latino. Despite being just seven miles southeast of downtown LA, South Gate is very far downwind of LA in terms of quality of life. The suburb has high levels of unemployment and poverty, high crime, and low levels of educational attainment. This is a particularly sad state of affairs when you learn that more than half of all households in South Gate have children under the age of eighteen living in them. One might easily assume that it is an emphatically unhappy place to be. But that is not so.

As I know from my own experience, the thing about growing up as a child living in poverty, is that your world is small and your frame of reference even smaller. And so it is perfectly possible to still have a fulfilling childhood if you've got the kind of parents who play football with you in the park, take you to libraries, make sure you've got clean clothes, cook you three good meals each day, teach you good manners and values and generally keep you on the straight and narrow. It is only when my younger brother and I look backwards in time from our 'grown up' lives of relative affluence, that we realise that our family was very poor.

South Gate also has one thing that transcends wealth and unemployment and education. That creates invisible bonds between people and provides opium for the masses of the local populace despite the underlying crime and gangs. And that is soccer. Playing soccer allows young people to reference and measure themselves not against their position in an economic hierarchy that is gamed against them from birth in favour of the kids from West LA, but by their conduct and skill on the soccer field. Soccer requires discipline, practice, dedication, teamwork, passion and a sense of fair play. All of these characteristics carry far more value in a society than they are given credence for. Big companies spend a lot of time at Colleges and Universities conducting 'milk rounds' to attract the most highly-educated students to work for them after they graduate. But there would a lot to be said for instead sourcing new talent from the soccer field, where they might see integrity, resolve and determination – all of them characteristics that once acquired become inherent, and which cannot be purchased or procured.

The earliest account of a form of soccer that you might reasonably recognise was first documented in the 1100's by Thomas Becket diarist William Fitzstephen. London youths would use an inflated animal bladder to play 'football' in the streets. By the 1300's most recorded instances of 'football' came from various declarations of it being banned: there were thirty bans recorded in England between 1314 and 1667 because the youth of the day created too much disorder and noise with their game. Once again life, much like Hollywood, recycles the same shapes of stories again and again. There is a joyful continuity that the authorities even as long ago as the 1300's looked with consternation at the activities being adopted by the youth and, in their discomfort, moved to ban them.

Modern soccer assuages geopolitical tensions that were previously exorcised through the combat of war, and it serves as a great reminder that regardless of the disagreeable actions of any individual government or autocrat, most citizens of the world and inherently good-natured. Our internal software is not programmed for conflict, but to avoid it in favour of good natured cooperation for the betterment of all. In that respect the soccer players of national teams are avatars who reach out to fellow global citizens to show that all humans can be united. Soccer is the world's common language and is an important catalyst for global peace.

It has never seemed to the outside world that the home of Baseball, Basketball and American Football has ever really opened its heart to soccer. As American soccer-cynics often gest: "Soccer is the sport of the future in America...and always will be!". However that is quickly changing. In the West Coast Latino and Hispanic communities are 'importing' their love of soccer. A 2018 Gallup poll found that 7% of Americans named soccer as their favourite sport to watch, compared to 4% just four years earlier. During that time all other major sports with the exception of hockey declined in popularity as a "favourite sport". And it is the young who are driving this change. Only 1% of those aged fifty five or over named soccer as their favourite sport, but the figure rose to 11% for those aged between 18-34. The times are changing.

My trip to South Gate was first-and-foremost because of the film that I was making, but it was also an opportunity to pay homage to a precept of Dr Samuel Johnson, who was scathing in his cutting assessment of travel writers who "tell nothing", because their method of travel leaves them to guess at the manners of the local inhabitants. Placed in a modern day context, Dr Johnson would be critical of any assessment of a place that was based on the areas that are sanitised to accommodate the demands of tourists for Instagram-friendly photos, but which bear little resemblance to the reality of life for most people who live there. For example it would be folly in the extreme to visit Hollywood and Beverley Hills and believe that you had in some way "experienced" LA.

South Gate did not have the visible signs of social discontent that I had expected, but the reason for my presence there with a film crew was illuminating. A British chain of soccer centres had built an enormous multi-pitch soccer facility on which several games of 5-a-side soccer could take place simultaneously. South Gate had been chosen as the location for its first big facilities in the USA. The facility allowed friends and families to bind together into teams and play in leagues and tournaments with other teams, with a lot of focus also on practice, training, spectating and socialising at the centre. The force behind opening the centre in LA was a visionary Scotsman who had become aware of the fact that whilst the demographics of South Gate meant it had great love for soccer, there were in fact no public spaces for young people to play games together.

This notion can seem rather unfathomable to people in Europe. Britain in particular is teeming with parks and playing fields and wide open green spaces that are freely available for the public to use. Local authorities go so far as to erect goal posts and to mark out pitches on fields for which they do not even charge people to use. They simply do it because that is what is done, and because it pays for itself several times over in terms of social utility and keeping the local youth amused. The local park on the housing estate of flat-roofed terrace houses where I grew up had a small play park, but attached to it was a huge field marked out for football and with two sets of goals. When the football season ended, the local authorities would take down the goals, but the local kids would then just remove their tops and pile them up to mark out where the goals used be, and the play continued. Come rain or shine, twenty or more young people could spend hours playing football without a care in the world – all they needed was for one of them to have brought along a football.

The South Gate soccer centre catered to players as young as three years old, but the majority of players were in their mid-teens and at that awkward 'inbetweener' stage of being neither boys nor men. All of them were Hispanic, and on a scorching hot day when my own head was pounding from the effects of drinking too many margaritas the night before, they were delighted to be able to play in front of a camera crew. Between play we would occasionally take a player aside for a short interview, much like a professional soccer player might be interviewed during half time or at the end of a soccer match. And they lapped it up because it made them feel like superstars.

Without question every single one of the young men had impeccably good manners. They were polite and courteous and respectful. These were without question good kids with dreams and ambitions despite having a rough start to their young lives. And yet the city didn't deem to create anywhere for them to freely play soccer?

After a lot of filming we took twenty or more of the young men into the soccer pavilion, where we had promised to buy them pizzas. They sat around two tables joking and laughing in that way that only teenage boys do. My motivation in buying the pizzas wasn't entirely selfless: I wanted a camera shot of fresh pizzas arriving, and happy players enthusiastically taking a piping hot slice whilst the cheese was still melting and runny. That would be our "money shot" and timing was everything since we would only have one chance to capture it. The two cameraman I was working with took a few practice shots and waited patiently for the pizzas. As they came into view the cameramen got into position and started rolling, relieved that this would be the last shot of a very hot and physically strenuous filming day. We all looked on as the pizzas were placed onto the two long tables, our breath held as we poised for the young men to immediately demolish the pizzas by all grabbing a slice. But they didn't.

Instead they did something that we had not expected and had not planned for. They all joined hands in a circle, closed their eyes, and started to pray. Not the kind of praying that happens because zealous parents are watching or because the soccer centre was within the control of a religious authority that demanded observance. It happened entirely because that is what the boys always did, it wasn't incited or forced upon them and it didn't need arranging of verbalising, it just was. These boys weren't even old enough to vote yet, but they were already good old-fashioned God-fearing Americans. Despite living in relative economic segregation these young men, who were overwhelmingly first-generation Americans, had bought entirely into the values of their country. Yet a codified version of national sentiment seemed to view the growth of their Hispanic and Latino community with suspicion. Certainly nobody was campaigning to maintain a field and mark out a few lines so that the young people of South Gate had somewhere that they could express their freedom by playing soccer for free.

When Ronald Regan referred to the prodigal "shining city" that metamorphosized his vision for America, he asserted that "If there had to be city walls, the walls would have doors and the doors would be open to anyone with the will and the heart to get there". Certainly these young men of South Gate had the will and the heart, but statistically their prospects were bleak despite their good character. The doors that they saw were not really open to them at all. And this brings us back to beta humans.

The notion of 'upgrading' the operating systems of the world refers to an all-encompassing endeavour. The easiest and most visible upgrades are those that also offer the best political return on investment, and that is the building of large-scale infrastructure that is accessible to all. Certainly this should be a key preoccupation of the world's first beta humans, as we shall explore later. But the greater challenge that must be solved in order for beta humans to emerge will be the upgrade of those operating systems that are entirely esoteric. It is a self-evident truth of humanity that the doors to self-improvement should be open to all. The path to self-betterment is never likely to be easy, in many ways it should be hard. But it should not be entirely impossible. The challenge for beta humans is to upgrade the world's operating system in a way that will elevate every human being, and to do it without deference to the kind of divisive political and social tribalism that has started to tear America apart and which has nearly sunk the American Dream altogether.

The case against the world's first beta humans arising from the crucible of technological innovation that is the West Coast of the USA rests on the great chasm that separates access to opportunity into 'have's' and the 'have nots' at the moment of birth. The notion of near-perfect meritocracy and equality in access to opportunities might seem like an impossible and idealist dream. But at one time so was the USA.

To end my West Coast trip I flew to a place where young people can boast plenty of fresh air and outdoor space: Seattle. Seattle might seem like an outlier compared to the areas around San Francisco and Los Angeles, which are faster-moving and home to more technological and contemporary innovations. But Seattle is important, because it is home to some world-changing businesses that matured long before the youthful titans of technology came to the fore. And it's these businesses that might give some insight about what the tech titans will look like at their full maturity – and whether they will be the architects of using new technologies to upgrade the operating systems of the world - or whether they will instead become "evil".

The first of those companies is Boeing, a company founded in Seattle in 1916, just thirteen years after the Wright brothers had invented the first successful airplane, thus giving the world a new technology that completely transformed all of humanity. After much wrangling of my contacts I had managed to arrange a private tour of the Boeing factory in Everett, just outside of Seattle, which is famous for being the largest building in the world by volume and covers an area that is bigger than Disneyland. The complex is so vast, that is has been rumoured to develop its own weather systems, with indoor clouds and even occasional rain.

The statistics that support its vastness are breath-taking. 30,000 people are employed by the factory, which functions much like a small city with dozens of cafes, a day care unit and a credit union. There are 2.3 miles of pedestrian tunnels underneath the factory so that workers can move around without affecting workflow, and the factory has over 1,300 tricycles that employees use to get around. The factory has over one million lightbulbs, and I can't help but feel sorry for whoever has the job of constantly changing them. Lightbulbs aside, Boeing is like a magic kingdom. Since 1968 the factory has built 4937 widebody planes, and as new middle classes emerge in the economies in Asia, demand for air travel is unprecedented. Boeing estimates that 42,730 new jets valued at $6.3 trillion will be needed over the next 20 years; a market in which Boeing has a dominant 43% market share.

Millennials might think that it was Google and Facebook that connected the modern world. But it was the airline industry which, in a period of just over one hundred years, turned a very big planet into a small global community. Thanks to aviation leaders like Boeing, cultures and experiences are exchanged, ideas are shared and entire nations became more prosperous through collaboration across global supply chains. More than one hundred thousand flights take off each day carrying more than 3.5 billion passengers and 50 million tonnes of cargo annually across a network of more than 50,000 routes. This connectivity supports 58 million jobs and $2.4 trillion of business. In short, aviation is the technology that truly elevates us.

In that respect the promise of technology-driven human betterment that is manifest in the West Coast of the

USA is nothing new. But the difference between Boeing and the new technology titans is that the overall impact of the airline industry has clearly been a net positive. But it is harder to draw this conclusion from the new wave of technology titans. Certainly Google has opened up the world to economic activity that would not otherwise have happened by connecting suppliers with businesses and businesses with customers, turning local markets into global markets, and combined with its constellation of other services, probably offers a huge net economic benefit to the world. Amazon Marketplaces has made it possible for retail entrepreneurs to run a business from a smartphone, sourcing products and selling them to customers worldwide without ever even having to touch them, reducing barriers to entry for retail entrepreneurs.

Except titans like Amazon have also undermined the traditional retail paradigm and precipitated the loss of thousands of jobs and billions in tax revenues. I don't know whether the economic contribution of Amazon to the world is net positive or not, but the fact that this is not obvious or self-evident is concerning in itself given the endemic role that Amazon plays in everyday life.

Then there is Uber. Uber for me is a bit like Starbucks. You don't really want to use it because you want to support the independent coffee shops to whom your money means a lot more. But when you find yourself in an unfamiliar place, you are always extremely happy to find one. Wherever I find myself in the world, if I know there is Uber, I can be less cautious, more adventurous and explore further, because I always know that if I get lost or suddenly need to get somewhere, Uber will find me and sort it out. The main reason that most people use Uber is simply because it is cheap. And in many places that quickly drew in swathes of customers. In London it put Black Taxi drivers into a perilous position. London Taxi drivers own their vehicles and are self-employed. Before they are allowed to drive they must spend years leaning and then pass a test on 'The Knowledge' – which is essentially the ability to navigate London more adeptly than satellite navigation but using only ones brain. Then suddenly an industry built on integrity and trusted values ever since 1897 was disrupted by Uber.

The trouble with Uber is that it is not creating new value through creative destruction, but stealing value that already exists with a modus operandi that harks back to economic imperialism. It is a net reducer of economic value. In 2015 analysts estimated that Uber passengers were paying only 41% of the actual cost of their trips, with the remainder being subsidised by the billions in funding that the company has raised. Not being a social enterprise, once that it has killed the competition, Uber will raise prices. That is as obvious as night following day. And when that eventually happens, customers will be paying the same price as before but for a service that is an inferior derivative of the honourable and upstanding tradition of the London Black Taxi. And then we will all question 'progress'.

The new wave of technology titans are therefore a bit like teenagers. Loud and brash and self-absorbed and obsessed with being liked. Whereas the more mature technology giants like Boeing are all grown up. And this, presumably, that means that Boeing has the maturity to contribute to the societies in which it relies for its customers, by paying its taxes? Well no. Over the ten years from 2008 to 2017 Boeing paid an effective federal tax rate of just 8.4% on $54 billion of US profits. In 2017 it paid an effective corporate tax rate of 13%, meaning it sheltered more than half of its profit from tax.

It does not bode well for the hope that eventually the 'technology teenagers' will contribute to the societies where they operate by paying a level of tax commensurate from the economic benefit that they extract, when a one-hundred-year-old 'technology stalwart' currently declines to do so. Even over a period of one hundred years, it seems that the draw of short term profits crowds out the opportunity to play a role in upgrading the operating systems of the world.

Which brings me on to another world-changing Seattle technology business that has already matured:

Microsoft. The story of Microsoft is well-known and its statistics are easily searchable. Its rise since being founded by a 20-year-old Harvard drop-out called Bill Gates in 1975 could be mapped into a diagram worthy of Kurt Vonnegut and easily applied to the technology titans that have followed in its wake. But what cannot be applied to those newer technology titans is something that we will call 'what Bill did next'. If beta humans do arise in the coming decade, Bill Gates could well become the father that they look to for guidance.

Bill Gates founded Microsoft in Albuquerque, but four years later moved it to his home territory of Seattle. Ostensibly this was because it was easier for Microsoft to find programming talent in Seattle than it had been in New Mexico, but I suspect it was simply because Mr Gates missed the many charms that Seattle has to offer. The small city centre retains an idiosyncratic character that feels missing from many other US cities. Pike Place Market and Kerry Park are what attract the tourists, but the main streets are filled with demure restaurants, cosy looking bars and small furniture stores. By total accident I found myself one night having dinner in a basement restaurant being entertained by an upbeat acoustic musician, and the next in a traditional steak restaurant eating the second best steak of my life (the best was in Kazakhstan).

But lounging in pleasant restaurants is only half of the Seattle lifestyle, because in Spring and Summer, the opportunities for outdoor activities are immense. Seattle has forty four state parks nearby and nineteen beaches. Bordered by water on two sides, it is also the perfect setting for water-sport activities like sailing. And within just a few hours are skiing and hiking at Mount Rainer, whale watching on the San Juan Islands, Mount St Helens volcano, rainforests lanes and mountains at Olympic Peninsula and also, bizarrely, a reconstructed Bavarian village at Leavenworth. That is of course if you can first survive the cold dark days of winter: a full ten percent of people in Seattle claim to suffer from Seasonal Affective Disorder.

So what did Bill do next? And why does it matter for prospective beta humans?

What Bill did next was the 'Bill And Melinda Gates Foundation'. The 'Gates Foundation' holds over $50 billion in assets and has a global aim to enhance healthcare and reduce extreme poverty. In 2006 Warren Buffet, who at that time was the world's richest man, pledged shares worth $1.5 billion to the Gates Foundation. Then in 2010 Gates and Buffet launched the 'Giving Pledge': a commitment by wealthy individuals to give away more than half of their wealth to causes including poverty alleviation, refugee aid, disaster relief, global health, education and medical research. There is only one requirement to be able to sign the giving pledge: you must be a billionaire. And so far more than 168 billionaires around the world have signed the Giving Pledge, including Tesla founder Elon Musk, Google co-founder Larry Page, eBay founder Pierre Omidyar, Facebook founder Mark Zuckerberg; as well as all three founders of AirBnB. Estimates are that the Giving Pledge will be worth $600 billion by

2022. That's equivalent to the entire annual budget of the government of Canada.

This matters for three reasons. Firstly because the Giving Pledge is the world's first truly coordinated attempt to channel technology wealth into causes that represent an 'upgrade' of society, such as the elimination of certain diseases. Secondly, because Governments are by nature cumbersome and imprecise and plagued by inertia, whereas the Gates Foundation takes a trailblazing approach that allows it to target its activities and attack the issues that matter with an unprecedented focus of strength. In 1988, 350,000 people in 125 countries were paralyzed by Polio every year. In 2007 the Gates Foundation contributed to a global campaign to eradicate Polio by 2020. In 2017 there were just 12 cases of Polio worldwide.

The third reason that 'what Bill did next' matters for beta humans is because the Gates Foundation and the Giving Pledge sets a clear precedent for a greater proportion of the proceeds of technology being

95

channelled and redistributed back into building a better world. It offers a glimmer of hope that the technology titans will ultimately be a force for good rather than for "evil". 'What Bill did next' shows us that once the teenage titans of technology start to mature, they may well precipitate the building of a new and upgraded world that is designed first and foremost to facilitate the betterment of all human beings. Empires can do good as well as evil, and the American empire offers a fast route for upgrading the worlds operating systems.

But neither is the world waiting idly for the USA to lead humanity into the future. The world's first beta humans may arise from the crucible of technology that is the West Coast USA. But they could equally rise from land that was once desert...

UNITED ARAB EMIRATES

Where I live in London there is a pub less than one hundred yards down the road. It's what many might call an "old man's pub" where the music is good but at a volume that does not intrude on conversations; the people working behind the bar are authentically welcoming, if also a little bit eccentric. The lights are dim and the furniture worn, but the beer is plentiful and served in big glasses, and the bill of fayre is the antithesis of the clean eating fad thanks to homemade classics such as pie and chips, battered cod with chips, shepherd's pie or gammon and eggs served with chips.

I have devised three tests of a good pub, which my local passes with flying colours. 1) Could you walk in alone and expect to engage a total stranger in genial conversation? 2) Can you conduct a conversation at a normal audible level without having to shout over music. 3) Does the pub serve good puddings?

The third point is one that can easily get lost in translation. My wife was born in Slovakia and lived in the South of France before we eventually moved in together in London in 2014. It was on one of our first ventures to our local pub, long before we got married, that my then-future wife was somewhat surprised when I mentioned that I was looking forward to "pudding".

"But why do you like pudding so much?" she asked.
"Because it's pudding!" I declared with enthusiasm.
"But it's so boring, I don't get the appeal?" she said.
"I'm not sure that we are compatible."

Thankfully there was no need to resolve our differences, and we were still able to get married two years later, because once that a piping hot homemade apple crumble was served to me drowning in bubbling hot vanilla custard, my wife declared that the meaning of 'pudding' had been lost in translation, and that in Slovakia, as in the USA, 'pudding' usually referred exclusively to a thick custardy dessert stuff.

As with so many idiosyncratic aspects of the English language, I could have made a half-hearted attempt to explain that in 'British English' pudding typically refers to any sweet dish served at the end of a meal, but can simultaneously also be used to refer to a savory steamed dish made with flour, such as Yorkshire Pudding, or to refer to a type of sausage, such as Black Pudding. But instead I resolved to enjoy my apple crumble with custard before it started to go cold.

My local pub originated during the Wars of the Roses in the 1460's when it was called The Hostel. Its name then changed in 1533 to The Red Cow – apparently a reference to a bar maid who was working there at the time. Its name changed again in 1766, and by 1811 it became the Town Of Ramsgate. It holds a unique position on the River Thames in Wapping next to 'Wapping Old Stairs', where at low tide you can still see the iron ring to which condemned pirates were once chained to drown as the river Thames rose with the tide.

British pub names are another idiosyncrasy that can't be found anywhere else in the world. Many pubs originated long before the majority of people were able to read, so every pub would hang a sign outside showing a unique picture. And much like modern brands choose composite or invented names such as 'Uber' or 'Google' so that they uniquely stand out from the crowd, pubs would typically choose pictures that were unlikely to be used by others nearby. So, when a group of sixteenth century workers agreed to meet at "The Swan With Two Necks", there was no doubt that their intended destination was the pub with a picture outside that depicted a swan that was collum endowed.

Some of the strangest pub names in Britain include 'The Hung Drawn And Quartered', located where medieval traitors were killed by that especially brutal punishment of hanging, drawing and quartering; 'The Bucket Of Blood', which refers to a supposed incident that took place 200 years ago when the pub landlord drew up a bucket filled with blood from the local well (a mutilated corpse was later found in the well); and perhaps the strangest pub name in Britain "The Jolly Taxpayer" in Portsmouth, which is early evidence of an enduring British fondness for comic irony.

My local pub, 'The Town of Ramsgate' was named after the Ramsgate fishermen who regularly unloaded their catch at Wapping Old Stairs. When in 1811 locals or sailors agreed to meet at 'The Town of Ramsgate', what they actually meant was "the pub on the Thames where the fishermen from the town of Ramsgate unloaded" - which the pub then adopted as its name.

I reflected on The Town Of Ramsgate as I recently tried to sum up Dubai in the United Arab Emirates. I tried to explain that there is a pub near my home that has been doing the same thing on the same site without interruption for well over five-hundred years. A good interior designer could visit that pub and take measurements of everything, source copies of the ephemera adorning the walls, match the décor and re-create an exact replica of the pub, but in Dubai. Except it simply wouldn't have the same feel. During more than five hundred years of serving beer to its punters The Town Of Ramsgate has developed its own esoteric character and identity that simply cannot be copied. It has an undefinable quality that you feel in your gut the moment that you walk inside.

Dubai, like much of the prosperous and growing Middle East, is the exact polar opposite of The Town Of Ramsgate. Dubai has risen from the desert and is building huge-scale infrastructure at an incredible pace. But it is also missing an undefinable quality that comes from age, and so provides a case study for beta humans about the balance between 'upgrading' and conserving, and the dangers of causing collateral damage to the seemingly innocuous things that are in fact reassuringly enduring rituals of our long heritage as human beings.

I arrived in Dubai during the beginning of a sweltering summer. The outdoor heat had reached over forty degrees Celsius and the hot breeze seared my eyes. Arriving in such scalding temperatures is it advisable to stay inside air conditioned buildings and taxis and to stay hydrated. It is very much not advisable to arrive with one of those hangovers that starts to set in even whilst you are still inebriated. Unfortunately, this is advice that I had not adhered to upon my arrival in Dubai. Over many years I had been using a British Airways credit card, and in doing so found that I had amassed over a quarter of a million Avios points – formerly known as AirMiles - that could only be redeemed on what is currently one of the world's most underwhelming international airlines: British Airways.

AirMiles are a curious unit of faux currency. Back in 2005 the same kind of fun-loving Economists who invented the 'Big Mac index' pointed out that the global stock of AirMiles in circulation was worth more than $700 billion, which was more than the total all of the US dollar bills in circulation, leading them to declare AirMiles to be "the world's biggest currency". But times have moved on since 2005. The 'Starbucks index' is now superior to the 'Big Mac index', and 'AirMiles' has been broken down into a multitude of new brands for turning loyalty into points-based currency. But they can still prove useful when you want to fly away for a few days to escape your worries without having to spend too much on flights.

One of the advantages of Dubai is that it is so well-served by so many excellent airlines such as Qatar and Emirates, that very few people actually want to fly from London to Dubai on British Airways. Or at least, very few people who are prepared to fly Business or First Class choose to do so with British Airways, because the amenities of their rivals are far superior. But that also means that when I found myself in the need of a break from the London summer, when the tube gets so hot that it starts to poach passengers in their own sweat and the streets are plagued by groups of slow-moving tourists, I found that I was able to use my points to book a First Class return ticket to Dubai for just £500.

Having paid my £500 to British Airways I had resolved to make the most of my First Class experience. When I was younger I had imagined that by my mid-thirties I would be successful, debt free and possibly even retired thanks to the series of companies and businesses I would have founded. But the reality of time is a leveler, and in truth my only previous experience of First Class was when walking through it to exit the plane having endured long haul flights in economy. And so I planned to extract as much value from it as I could, because there was a good chance that I would never get to fly First Class ever again.

Doing this is not difficult, because without exception, almost every other person that you see in Business or First Class seats on any airplane have not paid the full price for their ticket. Firstly, that's because airlines do not ever expect anyone to pay the full ticket price of a flight – the 'sticker price' as they say in the US. The 'sticker price' is merely an upper limit from which the airlines can offer entirely faux discounts. They offer discounts to companies booking many flights per year. Discounted seats to loyalty card holders and frequent flyers. And discounted seats to people like me, who have saved up enough Avios points to be able to redeem a seat for next-to-nothing and feel good about the fact I have paid £500 for an alleged £10,000 ticket, even though nobody has ever actually paid full price.

And the typical response of the people who travel in Business and First Class? To sweeten the deal even further by making the most of everything that is on offer. And because – at the time of writing - the British Airways First Class flights from London to Dubai lack the trimmings of its more plush rivals, there is just one way to make the most of the experience: by drinking the vintage wines and champagnes to beyond excess.

Now you might assume that the flight crew at British Airways would exercise some form of temperance over passengers drinking the seemingly never-ending supply of vintage wine and champagne. Except that is to forget that the flight crew are also British, and so not only will they allow such shamelessly proliferate overindulgence, but they will support and encourage it.

To my mind it is a classic example of the British psyche at work. British Airways could spend time and money equipping their planes with more gadgets and luxuries. They could turn their flight crews into subservient robots with no sass or personality. Or...they could simply make sure that every passenger is able to get so terrifically toasted on fine wines and champagnes that they will always have a good flight and – importantly – will keep coming back for more in spite of any inferiorities. Did I mention that I love British Airways?

And so I arrived in Dubai with my head in a dull ache and my throat dry after an extremely well-lubricated eight hour flight. The forty five degrees Celsius of heat in Dubai at the start of summer causes the gaseous water in the air to rise up very quickly, where it cools to below the dew point and condenses into water particles that get trapped suspended in the air, causing a thick fog of humidity that severely restricts visibility. And so my initial impressions were tempered not just by a vintage hangover, but poor visibility of the cityscape.

At the epicentre of downtown Dubai is the Burj Khalifa, the tallest building in the world, which at 828 metres tall stands more than twice as high as the Empire State Building in New York. It marks just one of many districts that can be easily accessed using Dubai's ubiquitous and inexpensive taxis. There are the glitzy skyscrapers of "Little Manhattan" around Dubai Marina; the densely rising construction of 'Business Bay' and the beautiful residences and exquisite hotels of Jumeirah and the Palm, as well as the booming district around the seven star Burj al Arab hotel.

Dubai got its first skyscraper building in 1979. Today it has hundreds and ranks third or fourth in the world behind Hong Kong and New York for the number of skyscrapers, depending on the height at which you start to deem a building to be a 'skyscraper'. The pace of development is so rapid, that even though New York and Hong Kong have a substantial lead in their number of skyscrapers, I am reluctant to quote figures, since whilst New York and Hong Kong have little space left, Dubai faces no geographical limitations to its expansion and has already shown how easily it can reclaim land from the sea and the desert as it continues to build.

By the end of 2021 construction could be complete on a new skyscraper that will be even taller than the Burj Kalifa, and I predict that in a short time, Dubai will claim the title for the highest number of skyscrapers of any city in the world, and that no other city will be able to reclaim that title again within current lifetimes.

The only thing that is more striking than the skyscrapers of Dubai is the rate of development. The scale and quality of the infrastructure that is being built to support future expansion is beyond exception. Infrastructure such as huge 8-lane roads and efficient intersections is being built not just for the next ten years, but for the next one hundred years and beyond. And it's here that Dubai offers its first inspiration for beta humans. Because if beta humans were engaged in the upgrade of the surroundings and the infrastructure that is used by everyone – the operating systems - then beta humans would certainly build it with many future generations in mind.

There is great precedent for the benefits of building infrastructure that is designed for future generations. The modern rail network in Great Britain, for example, (excluding NI) has 10,072 miles of track, and almost all of it was originally built during the booming Victorian era, when over 30,000 miles of track were laid. Almost all of the most used railway stations in Britain, including Kings Cross, Paddington and St Pancras stations in London, were designed and built by the Victorians, in 1851, 1852 and 1868 respectively.

Today Britain's creaking and ageing railway infrastructure is an archetypel example of why beta humans must commit to continual upgrades and improvement. Because the upgrades made to the British system over the last century have been wholly insufficient. Mere patches have failed to halt decline. So rail travel in Britain is now expensive, dirty and unreliable. It deprives hundreds of thousands of commuters of money and time with their families, and the high cost of rail travel often makes it inaccessible.

If the Victorian railway pioneers had been immediately followed by beta humans, then British railways today would be equivalent to the trains of the Shanghai Transrapid 'maglev'. The Shanghai maglev is a German-built magnetic levitation train that was the first high speed electric train in the world when it opened in 2004. A maglev train can reach 217mph in two minutes and has a typical speed of 268mph. When I first saw the Shanghai maglev I was on my way to the airport in 2017, feeling very tired after spending many weeks exploring the inner reaches of China. Out of my taxi window I spotted the most exquisitely-engineered movement of the maglev as it flew past at speed. You expect things to move slowly in densely built-up urban conurbations, but the maglev seemed to silently 'fly' past perfectly uninterrupted and completely oblivious to the slower world that it cut through. For a good few moments, I thought that I was inside a lucid dream.

And Dubai is not missing out on this opportunity to build and upgrade to the latest state-of-the-art railway infrastructure. Beta humans may observe plans for the

Dubai Hyperloop to connect Dubai and Abu Dhabi. The high speed transportation system would use electric propulsion to accelerate a passenger or cargo pod through a low pressure tube at speeds of up to 700mph. The train-like vehicle would levitate above the track, which is likely to be built on stilts above the ground next to the existing highway rather than occupying any new land. If successful – and given Dubai's form for defying expectations I do not doubt that it will be – then the Hyperloop would reduce journey times from over one hour down to just twelve minutes. Twelve!

Not only is Dubai infrastructure huge in both scale and ambition that it will serve the needs of future generations, but it is planned in an integrated way so that every aspect of the city works in symbiotic harmony with every other aspect. The buildings, the malls, the roads, the metro – everything is laid out according to a grand plan, and each part works and connects seamlessly with every other part in an intricately choreographed ballet of city-wide ambition.

But this is just the start of Dubai's plans to turn itself into 'the future city'. In 2017 the Dubai Roads and Transport Authority announced that flying drones carrying individual passengers could begin operation. By 2023 the huge $454m Dubai Water Canal project will open, adding kilometers of new waterfront and public spaces. By 2030, twenty five per cent of new buildings will be 3D printed. And by that same year a quarter of all journeys will be in autonomous vehicles.

I contemplated this progression of 'the future city' as I arrived on the observation deck on the 125th floor of the Burj Kalifa. I paced the perimeter of the building whilst trying to avoid walking into the photos of the throngs of tourists. The white humidity had blown out the horizon, and so with no distant view most tourists were trying to awkwardly angle themselves against the glass exterior of the building to capture the view of Dubai's famous 'dancing fountains' 555 meters below.

Even on a clear day, to look out on Dubai is actually very hard to do, even from the dizzying heights of the

Burj Kalifa, because Dubai's glisteningly new districts of shiny new skyscrapers are spread out miles apart from each other. So when you do look out, what is striking and immediately noticeable, is that there is a huge amount of land that is still to be developed. The vista evokes the same feeling you would have looking out on Manhattan in 1901 in the full knowledge that just one hundred years later the skyline would be crammed with the windy corridors of the vast jungle of tall buildings, each paying their homage to the driving forces of cathedral capitalism as they stretch to compete for air space in a Tetris of concrete, steel and glass.

That is not to say that the completed developments of Dubai are not awe-inspiring. But some of the earlier architecture lacks the elegance of cities like London, where many new skyscrapers stand alone in the horizon and so are designed as much as huge pieces of urban art or sculpture as they are for their utilitarian purpose. The 'poster boy' tall building in London used to be what is affectionately known as 'the Gherkin', because of its unique form: it is essentially an elongated, curved shaft with a rounded end, that is reminiscent of a stretched egg or gherkin. It was built in 2003 at a cost of £200 million, and put up for sale just three years later with a price tag of £630 million. The huge appreciation in value was attributed to its status as an iconic symbol of London that is as recognizable around the world in silhouette as St Paul's Cathedral or Big Ben.

This actually creates a problem that is also worthy of note for beta humans. The notion of major buildings 'pioneering a new future' and becoming 'iconic brands' means that anything which follows must show either deference to them, or become a function of them. A pioneering new vogue in design has its original pioneers who create demand for that certain taste, and then rather than blaze their own idiosyncratic trail, subsequent architects (and artists too since architects and artists share this common problem) are required to create work that either directly emulates this taste, or which is valid only because of its relative stature. It is not so different to the many artists of Italy at the time of the Renaissance, who spent much of their careers engaged in the production of beautiful masterpieces that spoke to the 'glory of Catholicism', because it was the Catholic church who held all of the purse strings, and religious imagery was what they saw and what they wanted. Architects are faced with the task of trying to 'reinvent' something that has already been clearly defined by popular acclaim, and invariably, this limitation most often leads them to having to take what is already in vogue and simply make it bolder, brasher and more shocking. This 'brash and shocking' vogue is not always a bad thing. Absurd and shocking can also be usefully provocative. Having grown up in a very small town in the heart of the deprived former industrial heartlands of England, when I first travelled to London by myself for the first time aged 19 and discovered the shocking and brash work of artist Damien Hirst, my eyes were opened to the endless possibilities and absurdities of life. It smashed my ideas and preconceptions to pieces and forced me to put them back together in a way that would never be the same again. It changed my outlook during formative years.

This can be a problem for beta humans seeking to upgrade the operating system of the world. Right now the architectural vogue manifests itself in various forms of steel and glass. But in 1960's Britain it manifested itself in concrete towers that history has since judged very poorly. The 'upgrades' of the 1960's that these concrete towers represented were entirely illusory. Nobody stopped to question the merits of these concrete monstrosities and the misery that they would later cause, because each new tower was a function of the much lauded 'progress' of the one that came before. It offers a lesson in the perils of 'blind progress' that beta humans must heed before 'upgrading' anything!

In Dubai you can't help but feel that the overwhelming goal in the early 2000's was to 'get them built and make them tall' rather than to 'make them beautiful'. But it is completely beyond doubt that this has since changed, and Dubai can be forgiven some of its earlier architecture as a necessarily evil for getting it to where it is today. The city is commissioning handsome new buildings of great architectural and artistic merit.

As I continued my walk around the perimeter of the viewing floors of the Burj Kalifa, I stumbled into a family of Chinese tourists standing in front of a huge green screen, their faces glistening from the lights that were being shone upon them by a photographer who was apparently taking a souvenir photo. I have never understood these 'green screen' souvenir photos. My wife and I once lined-up atop The Peak in Hong Kong so that the resident photographer could capture a photo of us with the iconic night time skyline of Hong Kong and Kowloon in the background. Our own camera simply wasn't sensitive enough to capture the detail of our faces in the foreground and the fairground of bright lights and tall buildings in the background. So against normal judgement we paid a photographer who took a beautiful picture. It's one of our favourite photographs and it says – "we were there" – because we were!

But at many of the tall buildings that I have recently visited – The Shard in London, the Shanghai Tower, the International Commerce Centre in Hong Kong – the 'green screen' photo souvenir seems to be becoming ubiquitous and, even more surprising, tourists seem to queue up for hours just to get their photo taken. Why? What is the point in ascending some of the tallest buildings in the world just to have your family picture taken in front of a green screen, onto which the view-from-the-top is then digitally superimposed into a photo for you collect as you leave? You could literally have stayed at home and saved yourself the trouble by asking any teenager with basic Photoshop skills to do the same for you. Nobody would ever be any the wiser!

I apologized to the Chinese tourists for ruining their photograph, and continued to ponder on the level of central planning required for the 'grand united vision' that would be required to create the great infrastructure of the 'future city' below. 'Grand plan' infrastructure is by no means anything new. It is a well-trodden tale than in the 1850's London suffered 'the great stink'. For a long time London's streets had been piled-high with the faecal waste of humans and horses and dead animals. Almost all human waste and industrial affluent found its way into The Thames in such quantity that the river was biologically dead. Then a series of prolonged hot summers heated the Thames into a soup of detritus. By 1850 the smell was causing great annoyance to the privileged Members of Parliament and Lords sitting in the Palace of Westminster. And so as with so many of the world's issues, once that the rich and powerful started to feel the sting – or in this case the stink - it quickly became not just acceptable, but an imperative to spend public money on solving the problem. So Victorian engineer Joseph Bazalgette was called in to design and construct a sewer system for London, which was constructed between 1859 and 1870 from 260 million bricks that were held in place with the strongest mortar known to man. The new sewer system was 550 miles long and was a huge undertaking. It brought the biologically-dead River Thames back to life, ended the stench and, more importantly, saved tens of thousands of Londoners from death by cholera.

At the time London had a population of two million people, but Bazalgette designed the sewers to accommodate a city of four million people – twice the size that was necessary. The apocryphal story goes that members of Bazalgette's engineering team presented him with the final plans for a sewer system that would perfectly serve the London of the day. Bazalgette looked at the plans, approved of the design and layout, but requested one major change: "the size – double it!". And so a city of two million people got a sewer system fit for a city of four million people, and in fact that same sewer system to this day serves a city that has a population of over eight million people. It took until 2018 before work started on the Thames Tideway, the first major sewer upgrade project to represent more than a mere iterative patch onto Bazalgette's original system.

Beta humans must similarly take responsibility for planning for future population growth. And 'grand plan' infrastructure will play a role. But it would be a mistake to assume that to become beta humans is as simple as creating new boulevards and buildings. Much like the unwritten British constitution, the vast majority of the 'operating system' upon which we build our lives is entirely esoteric. We are enthral to its conventions and precedents even when they are no longer serving the wider human interest. And nowhere is that more clear than when it comes to property prices.

Between 1997 and 2016 the median price paid for a home in England leapt by 259%, whilst earnings rose by only 68%. In 1997 house prices were between three and four times the average salary. By 2016 they were between seven and eight times. Similar trends throughout the Western world means that the first generation of potential beta humans are condemned to working more, spending more on their income on rent and mortgage payments, delaying having children and not having time to participate in their local community.

This 'operating system' of the property market in the UK, and indeed in most Western countries, is thus not fit for the modern era and is in serious need of upgrade. Beta humans must upgrade this operating system so that adequate and spacious housing is more readily accessible and available to young couples. At present individuals have become slave to the operating system that is the property market. Beta humans must innovate a more subservient property system that is designed first and foremost to provide adequately for the health and happiness and family ambitions of future generations – not for speculation and the accumulation of unearned wealth. A successful upgrade of this operating system will also enable and liberate future generations to also become beta humans themselves.

The property market is thus highly symptomatic of how the modern operating system of our society has become misaligned with the higher purpose of human betterment. When I was a child in the 1980's, often my mother would dispatch me to our local independent store that we called 'Davids'. David was the name of the shopkeeper. I would pick up the items that my mother had written for me on her list, and then at the till, I would ask to pay "on tick". "On tick" was basically credit. If as a family you found yourself with no money, David would let you take anything that you needed as long as you paid it back at a rate of a few pounds each week and didn't let the amount that you owed him start to get too high. There were no credit checks, no contracts, no interest rates. David was not even making a great living as a small shop owner. But allowing customers to buy "on tick" was just the 'done thing' for a small shopkeeper on a poor housing estate.

My family got by and, unbelievably by today's standards, my parents had four children. We had a three bedroom house in which my parents had one bedroom, my sister another, and my two brothers and I shared the third. But we never really noticed that we were poor, because my father always worked, we almost always had food, and our mother was stay-at-home so we were always greatly cared for. There was almost always time for my father to read us a bedtime story or to spend some time with us in the local park. Today people are theoretically richer and better off than they were in the 1980s. But is it better to measure wealth by the colossal salary needed to buy a good quality family home? Or would a better measure be the level of freedom and financial latitude that families have left over after paying their living costs to use to enjoy their life, liberty and the pursuit of happiness?

This is one of the biggest challenges that beta humans must solve across the West. In Britain today, as in many Western nations, a child might have two parents working, with a seemingly healthy combined income, but their childhood experience will likely be one of anonymous day care and of frantically busy and tired-out parents who they rarely get to see.

Is this really the operating system that we want?

There is a real risk that those children will miss out on early life experiences that will not be nearly as enriching or nourishing as my siblings and I enjoyed whilst living in relative poverty in the 1980s. Across the West, as next generations of children get older, I wager with total dismay that political stability will diminish as they – the first generation of prospective beta humans - dare not even dream of owning property or having a large family, and therefore vote for anything that offers an alternative to the status quo. Far from becoming beta humans, this generation could all too easily usher in political parties with authoritarian tendencies toward the imposition of myriad rules and controls in the erroneous pursuit of improving the prospect of individuals for whom the "status quo" offers nothing.

In 2020 a report by Deutsche Bank predicted that the Millennials will usher in an "age of disorder" as they attain greater levels of influence within governments and corporations and use it to redistribute wealth away from older generations. The report notes that if life does not become more economically feasible for Millennials as they age, it could prove a turning point for society and start to change election results and thus change policy away from the principles that created the stable conditions for human prosperity. It would be a tragedy if the epoch of the beta humans were to be usurped by such a harmful reversion, but it looks likely.

This is highly relevant. Because whilst 'the future city' of Dubai is easily lauded as a beacon of light in the Middle East – a 'shining city by the sea' to paraphrase

Matthew 5:14 (and also Ronald Reagan) – it is also important to note some of the aspects of Dubai that loom much larger in popular sentiment: that the United Arab Emirates, for which Dubai is the 'poster boy' city, is openly discriminatory and politically authoritarian.

The UAE is thus a place of huge contrast and open moral conflict. It is simultaneously conservative whilst also being one of the most liberal countries in the Gulf. It has one of the highest Internet penetration rates in the entire Arab world, whilst also extensively filtering online content to prevent sedition. In cities like Dubai there is an extremely vibrant night time party scene - though I'm afraid that I am neither good-looking, rich or young enough to join it for the purposes of research! And in a country that is staunchly conservative, there is a very high number of young and extremely well-presented Western women working in the 'escorting' industry, which is perhaps to be expected with highly affluent cities like Dubai where 85% per cent of the population are aged 45 or under and 70% are male.

The lessons for beta humans are complex and help to emphasise why becoming beta humans is so important. But they can also be summarised quite simply: If the status quo of the current operating system of the West is failing the next generation, then do not be surprised if in the future that same generation starts to re-weigh their liberal democratic values against their own daily reality, and decide that they could in fact accept living with political authoritarianism. Iterative patches to the operating systems of the West have created a system that is leaving too many people behind. If we do not succeed in becoming beta humans, then the risk is not that Western nations become stagnant, but that they retrench into expedient and regressive ideologies. In this respect becoming beta humans is not just about manifesting an idealised future. It is also about avoiding and preventing the descent of humanity which could occur if Western nations do not upgrade their operating systems fast enough to satisfy citizens.

Beta humans must not be so arrogant as to assume that the primacy of liberal democracy guarantees its protection. Ronald Reagan often spoke about a 'shining city'. Reagan proclaimed that he envisioned "a tall, proud city built on rocks stronger than oceans, wind-swept, God-blessed, and teeming with people of all kinds living in harmony and peace; a city with free ports that hummed with commerce and creativity. And if there had to be city walls, the walls had doors and the doors were open to anyone with the will and the heart to get here. That's how I saw it, and see it still."

Today it is Dubai that is becoming Regan's shining city. And in doing so it is showing that liberal democracy is not a prerequisite for its success. If Bazalgette were alive today, he wouldn't be in London, but in Dubai.

CHINA

Most people are fundamentally good and courteous. Our internal software has been programmed by years of evolution to recognise that a disposition for cooperation, rather than conflict, generally leads to better outcomes. This has been true for generations, even whilst the operating systems – either by accident or by design – have evolved to erect barriers to the genial behaviours that have long been the bedrock of a good society. This has become self-evident in Britain, where even recent immigrants bemoan and lament that the famously polite courtesies and manners of British society that they had so envied and hoped to become a part of, have substantially diminished in modern times.

More worrying is that there is now a whole generation who have never known 'good society' at all. The 'Millennials' are faced with an almost hopeless situation of never being able to buy a property or have a good job or start a family or to own a nice car. And faced with the near-impossibility of these basic human wants, their currency of measurement of a successful life is not their comfort or achievements, but their 'likes'. Whether something can be posted onto Instagram seems to be one of the main drivers of Millennial decision-making. Presenting the image of an interesting and exciting life is more highly-regarded than actually living a life - and who can blame this generation for deciding to give up on the impossible dream of property ownership, and instead spend what little money that they have on 'postable' experiences.

This creates a kind of 'arms race' for what people post on social media: a kind of 'life bingo' where a typical millennial has to 'tick off' a number each time that he or she makes a particular post. Sunset picture on a backpackers beach in Thailand: tick. Nice meal out with lots of friends for your birthday: tick. Selfie after you've just finished a tough workout? Tick.

This brings us to China. China is an emerging Empire . The country is home to twenty per cent of the world's population who are challenging the superpower monopoly that the United States maintained throughout the second half of the Twentieth century; and my plan upon arriving in China was to explore the East and Northwest of this vast country, starting in Beijing before progressing to Lijiang, Hangzhou and then finishing in Shanghai. It was an itinerary I had chosen to take in the extremes of the old and the new in China.

In 1999 a major British DIY chain started opening stores in China and had some initial success, before making a hasty retreat as the Chinese customers proved that they did not have a zeal for DIY home improvement. The reasons for this failure were widely attributed to two factors: the first being that the lowest minimum wage in China, which is set regionally, is approximately $170 per month, which means that anyone who can afford to make home improvements can also easily afford to have someone do the work for them rather than spending their weekends engaged in tiresome DIY. The second reason, is that in general, Chinese people do not place so much value in having a showroom-style home to impress their friends and neighbors. In China a home is more of a practical place for sleeping and family, whereas most social occasions take place out of a home. Because why have a dinner party when you can eat in a restaurant for the same cost but without the hassle of the cooking and cleaning?

This means that Chinese spending habits differ greatly from the West. A Chinese person is more likely to spend their disposable income on designer clothes and watches, jewelry and nice cars and other displays of status that will be seen away from the home, rather than on a stylish new kitchen or a designer sofa. And much like the Millennials of Britain and other Anglo-Saxon nations, this same attitude spills over greatly into social media. In China if you are young and you are not a prolific user of social media to display your latest outfit, purchase, meal, travels and adventures, then, quite frankly, you do not exist. It took many centuries of human societal development and advancement before Descartes postulated "cognito ergo sum" ("I think therefore I am") to neatly surmise what defines human existence as sentient beings. But just 400 years later "I post therefore I am" has perhaps became a more accurate summation of contemporary human existence.

But whilst the Millennials of the West turn to the fleeting escapism and synthetic satisfaction of social media as a refuge from an operating system that is failing them, many of their counterparts in China are enjoying considerably more prosperous circumstances. In the year 2000 just four percent of the urban population in China were considered middle class in terms of price-adjusted purchasing power. By the year 2022 that number will rise to seventy six percent. 76%!

And whilst households of the United Kingdom and United States are encumbered by levels of household debt relative to GDP of 87% apiece, in China that figure is a mere 40%. This means that the Chinese have to spend less of their income servicing their mortgages and other debts, and they also have the room to borrow more money if they need to make a bigger purchase.

I landed in Beijing contemplating the relationship between Empires and progress. Winston Churchill once made the supposition that "the Empires of the future will be Empires of the mind", and by that definition, surely the Twentieth century Empire of the United States exceeds the power zeniths of all empires?

My American friends feel uncomfortable about talk of an "American Empire". The United States is built on stories of rebelling against a global empire to claim independence and the freedom to pursue "life, liberty and happiness"; and so the notion that the USA has since become an empire in its own right proves hard for them to process. But if we set aside the long history of occupying or exerting undue influence and control over other countries, and the smattering of strategic territories spread thousands of miles from the USA in the Pacific Ocean (Guam is over seven thousand miles from the mainland USA), and also ignore the most technologically advanced military in human history and the brutality of a country with four and a half percent of the world's population housing twenty two percent of the world's prisoners; then what remains is that the USA exerts a monumentally huge influence over the modern world – a lot of it using 'soft power'.

Beta humans should take note, since this was the true brilliance of the United States in the Twentieth century. It is the reason that many of the world's population harbour a long term desire to live in the USA and for their children to be born as Americans. The cultural exports of the USA dwarf every other nation on earth except perhaps for Britain. Films, music, television, food, cars, brands, everyday technologies, innovations and a general attitude that "hell yeah we can do it" – the USA exports all of this to the world, and the world laps it up. America is the physical embodiment of Winston Churchill's esoteric "empire of the mind".

This contrasts to the more tangible former British Empire, which gave the world engineering, trade...and violence. Britain believed that a superior civilization was on offer and expected the natives to be grateful. When they frequently were not – from the American

War of Independence to Mau-Mau – Britain resorted to war. A good case has been made by some excellent historians and writers that much of Britain's Empire was built accidentally through a mix of canny pre-emption, economic appetite and political hubris in the face of all evidence that an Empire was often costly, pointless and vicious. One of the worst instances of mindless viciousness came in 1856 when a British force captured Peking (Beijing) and burned and looted the Emperor's Summer Palace, destroying what many regarded as one of the seven wonders of the world.

I contemplated this as I arrived at the restored remnants of the Summer Palace just outside Beijing. A small part of the Palace has now been converted into a very passable boutique hotel, with a private underground cinema fit for an Emperor. But what lessons can China offer to beta humans? Could China really challenge the colossal soft power of the American Empire and channel it into becoming the world's first beta humans?

Certainly China has performed an economic miracle that has lifted eight hundred million of its own people out of poverty and into the comforts of the middle class. And it is exerting international influence with increasing confidence and imperialism. China made $86 billion in loans to finance over 3,000 infrastructure projects in Africa between 2000 and 2014, creating jobs and providing opportunities for skilled developments that reduced poverty at an unprecedented speed and made aid-based Western efforts look impotent. In 2014 the USA pledged to invest $14 billion in Africa over the next decade. China promised $175 billion. $175 billion! The sheer scale of this ambition is a worthy lesson for beta humans in their pursuit to improve, build and upgrade the world's operating systems.

The Summer Palace is a collection of buildings, bridges and follies spread around a manmade mirror lake. It was used by the Emperor to escape the claustrophobic Forbidden City during the searing heat of the summer months, and remains a place of relative peace and tranquility at the break of dawn. However as the sun continues to rise, the Summer Palace quickly becomes overrun with tourists from all over China, many of them in colossal groups, all moving together in vast herds behind a flag-carrying leader. Ironically it is the soft power of the United States that has created one of the cultural problems that China faces today. There are now so many newly-middle-class Chinese people that they all want to fill their social media accounts with pictures showing what all of those American movies and television programmes have encouraged them to aspire to: 'Instagrammable' experiences - although in China the preferred social media channel is 'WeChat'.

The trouble is that China does not have enough monuments and places of beauty and interest for the masses to travel to and experience. Or rather, it does not have enough places that are 'officially designated' as somewhere that can be visited. And this supply problem means that every location on every single tourist trail becomes completely overwhelmed with people, each trying to 'take in' and feel the history or beauty or importance of a place. Except the number of fellow travellers crowding every single vista and photo opportunity makes this objective entirely impossible.

And it's not just the 'famous' sights and experiences that have an air of the synthetic about them. Some of the 'infamous' ones do too. Take for example the handful of street food markets selling foods that most Westerners would not contemplate: insects, bugs, snakes, still-moving scorpions and grasshoppers. These markets are often-covered by television travel programs under the guise of "look how strange the food is that they eat here". And that's not entirely inaccurate – if you visit one of these markets, you will encounter Chinese people chewing on an Octopus tentacle or crunching a grasshopper. But you'll see Western tourists doing it too. Because the markets aren't selling dishes to quell the appetite, they're selling novelty 'foods' for tourists to photograph for social media. What you certainly won't encounter is locals queuing up to fill their baskets with a weekly shop, or young Chinese buying their lunch when there is a McDonalds nearby. And yet a quick look on TripAdvisor and you'll find many Western tourists waxing lyrical about an "authentic cultural experience". What nonsense.

The Chinese have responded to the immense domestic demand for 'experiential tourism' by creating some brand new historical and beautiful places to visit, which is illuminating of the Chinese mindset. The Summer Palace for example, is an excellent restoration of its original form and elevations, particularly as most of the original contents of the Summer Palace have long been spirited away to the British Museum in London.

The Forbidden City in Beijing is truly unique in the world, and was once the heart of the world's earliest sophisticated civilization at a time when Europe was still in the dark ages. But one should not tell oneself as you walk around the glorious Forbidden City that what you are looking at has stood since 1420. Most of the buildings of the Forbidden City are made of wood. That makes them very easy to catch fire, and there are over fifty fires on record during the Ming and Qing dynasties. The most devasting fire was in 1644, when a peasant uprising overthrew the Ming dynasty and burned the entire Palace to ruins that took over one hundred years to rebuild. Then in 1923 the Palace caught fire again, but when firefighters came to the rescue, they were forbidden from entering without the permission of the Emperor. It took nearly two hours to find the Emperor, who still refused to let firefighters enter the Palace. He called a meeting to discuss the issue and eventually let the firefighters in, by which time the northwest of the Forbidden City was in cinders. You can't help but think that the Emperor would feel kinship with many of the leaders of today's slow-to-react and bureaucratic Government agencies.

This is not to say that other ancient nations have not also razed and rebuilt buildings of historic importance. Many of the grand houses and castles of Britain sit atop earlier iterations, and some of the more fanciful buildings of British history are gone entirely, such as Henry VIII's 1538 'Nonsuch Palace' which was demolished and sold off in bits in 1683 to pay the gambling debts of its new owner. Thankfully the Great

Wall of China has not suffered this fate of being carted away to use as building materials elsewhere, though such is its' precarious position on the top ridges of mountains and hills, that I can't see that it would be easy to ever do so. Like most Chinese monuments, the Great Wall has been extensively refurbished along the sections that tourists are allowed access to, but such is it's huge vastness, that any refurbishment cannot have amounted to much more than shoring up the sides with fresh mortar and making sure that the paths were clear.

I travelled out from Beijing toward an open section of the Great Wall before daylight so as to arrive there well ahead of the tour groups. The great thing about tour groups, if you're not in one, is that they can only go as fast as their slowest member, and so they invariably don't get started too early so as to cater to those who like a slow start and a long breakfast. I arrived at a section of the Great Wall, parked up and bought tickets, where I was informed that I could hike up to the wall – taking about one hour – or use the equivalent of a ski lift. So I boarded the ski lift as the first passenger of the day, and as the sun began to rise, enjoyed the coolness of the morning air. As the ski lift progressed upward and I anticipated becoming overwhelmed by the sight of the wall as the sun rose beyond it, I was instead overwhelmed by another of my senses. There is a particular type of tree called Pyrus Calleryana, which is also otherwise known as the 'ornamental pear'. It is native to China, but was exported to the world in the 1950's as the urban designer's tree of choice because they are small and neat and produce cute white flowers.

The Pyrus is also responsible for the release of a very distinct smell. And there is no sensitive way to put this: it smells like ejaculate. Apparently this is to attract insects for the purposes of cross pollination, something which is fairly common in nature. There's apparently even an entire subset of stinky plants called carrion flowers that mimic the stench of decay to attract bugs that usually feast on the corpses of rotting animals. But when you fly across a forest of Pyrus first thing on a dewy morning as they are waking for the day, you will certainly know about it as the taste of the distinctive smell hits your throat and makes you want to gag.

I was relieved to disembark the ski lift and find myself on a deserted Great Wall without another human being in sight. I had been prepared to be dazzled by the scale of this engineering feat, but I had not been prepared for its overall handsomeness and magnificence. It truly is one of the most remarkable things to behold, and when I walked along it, across narrow winding sections, through tall guard houses and up and down uneven steps, occasionally I would look over my shoulder to see the Great Wall behind me, snaking across the very tops of the mountains for as far as the eye can see in either direction. It really is magical.

You can spend days hiking along the Great Wall. I must have walked for quite a few miles in either direction, but by mid-morning the crowds and souvenir sellers had started to arrive, and it was starting to feel a bit like walking down Main Street at Disney Land, so I left before the tourists could dampen my feelings of satisfaction, and by joyous happenstance, I discovered that a toboggan ride had been built to take tourists back down the mountain – I mean why not! I paid a few extra Yen and found myself hurtling down the hill pretending that I was ten years old again. It was great.

China is reinstating and opening new swathes of the Great Wall all the time, so there's now more to visit than ever before. In fact the authorities are going even further to quell the appetites of the masses for that perfect social media photo, by creating even more sights interest far beyond the Great Wall, as I observed when I left Beijing and flew to Lijiang.

Budget domestic flights in China are as tiresome and inhuman as any others around the world. In fact it is a miracle of modern humanity that airports of all sizes and in all countries have managed to attain such homogeny in their ability to suck out all of the joy from the experience of travelling. I took my first flight when I was nine years old and I still remember it clearly. It was our first family holiday to the hitherto mythical

146

place of "abroad". We didn't know what to expect of "abroad" so my parents took extra precautions and packed a freezer bag full of enough food to last a fortnight, and my younger brother and I packed our suitcase with crisps and cereal packets. In preparation for the flight my brother and I had also both been bought new 'Reedok' (that's not a typo) trainers from the local Saturday market, as well as matching tracksuits. We climbed onto the 'AirTours' plane behind many other families, each pausing to have their photos taken as they excitedly ascended the stairs.

I was reminded of my maiden flight to Menorca as I waited to board my domestic flight from Beijing to Lijiang. There were many groups on the flight, most of whom seemed to be domestic tourists. And far from exhibiting the exasperated nonchalance that is typical of those boarding and taking a seat on an aircraft, they boarded with something that I can only describe as excited anticipation. It turned out that for many of the people in these groups, who ranged in age from forty upwards, this was going to be their first ever experience of flying. Can you imagine not having flown until you reached your forties? I have an old suitcase that is covered in gaffer tape and makes a noise as you pull it like when you stick a playing card into the spokes of a bicycle, because it has travelled and survived over quarter of a million flying miles over the last fifteen years. Flying is just second nature in the West. But the excitement on the faces of grown men and women as they took off for the first time, and their clapping cheers as the plane landed a few hours later, was a delight to behold, and harked back to the days when flying was a pleasure to be enjoyed.

Lijiang is the kind of Chinese city where you can make a realistic attempt to avoid seeing any other Western faces. The area has evidence of being occupied by the late Paleolithic sapiens over one hundred thousand years ago, and the Baisha Old Town was established in 658AD. The Old Town was once the center of silk embroidery in China and the most important place on the ancient silk road that runs from Burma to Lijiang before progressing on to Tibet, then Iran, through the

Fertile Crescent and ultimately to the Mediterranean sea. The Old Town is the most preserved ancient town in China and a UNESCO world heritage site. So naturally, the Chinese have turned the original buildings into small shops stacking tacky souvenirs and cashmere scarves, which the tens of thousands of Chinese tourists seem to buy without question, and the area immediately outside the Old Town is now surrounded by the ubiquitous Burger King, McDonalds and KFC.

Maybe it's because there are so many people to feed and water, but the Chinese don't seem to think that a location is sufficient as a destination for tourism until it has been turned into a Disney-style spectacle, with coach parks and visitor centers and food courts. Perhaps even more curiously, it was apparent that the many shops of the Old Town had been mandated a single piece of music to dutifully play on tortuous loop.

Naturally as a UNECSO site the town does also attract a few hardy Western tourists, and so using the English-language TripAdvisor tends to rank the local restaurants that are favoured by the occasional backpacker. I walked into one of the top ranked restaurants above a small shop to be greeted by a scene of austerity – just a few tables and chairs and a shelf full of books in various languages. A young woman emerged and assured me that this was indeed a restaurant and that it was indeed open and that she was both the owner and the cook. Craving some greasy carbohydrates I ordered an American-style burger and tucked into a thoroughly satisfying meal accompanied by a very nice cold beer.

After my meal I ventured behind the bookcase to find the young woman sat at a table with two young children and her husband. They were sat having a family dinner of noodles whilst watching a small television set. I realized that this restaurant was also their home – the one room restaurant was their main residence and presumably they slept there at night too. It wasn't that I had wondered into their home and they had been hospitable, but that their restaurant and their home were one and the same thing. And suddenly when faced with the reality that real people were living real lives in the

150

Old Town, possibly in the same small houses that their families have occupied for generations, I regretted my dismissive attitude that the central authorities had turned the Old Town into a Disney-style attraction. I couldn't help but think that whilst there is no doubt that the hundreds of thousands of tourists visiting Lijiang must have improved the family's income, their once quiet town high up at an altitude of 2,416 meters at the foothills of the Himalayas was now being overwhelmed by them. For all their financial gain, I had to wonder if the family were really any better off as a result?

There is a line in Abraham Lincoln's Gettysburg address about "Government of the people, by the people, for the people" which speaks volumes of the need for humility and humanity from those who govern. But in China it is hard to determine whether this sentiment is shared. Certainly the majority of Chinese people are considerably better off since the country adopted de facto capitalism. But you also get the sense that progress has been geared for the amorphous masses and not for the individual human beings who have been swept along by the reforms and the changes. The sense is that the unelected central bureaucracy decides what is best for all people, and then makes them take the appropriate medicine, regardless of how they feel about it. This gives individuals very little scope to exercise free control over their own destiny and lives. Individuals are like small boats, they are all lifted by a rising tide, but if that tide comes in great waves they are left to the mercy of their own devices to grip on tightly.

This is where China offers important lessons for beta humans. Modern human history is littered with the consequences of nations who have attempted to upgrade their operating systems without the full consent of citizens. Upgrades without a democratic mandate were responsible for some of the greatest human tragedies of the Twentieth century. Mao's 'Great Leap Forward' led to 45 million unnecessary deaths. Stalin's 'Five Year Plan' caused six to seven million deaths from starvation. And whilst the world has since convened into a system interconnected and interdependent operating systems that should avoid a repeat of these human tragedies, these past instances serve as a cautionary tale against 'upgrading' without full consent.

To succeed, beta humans must upgrade the world's operating systems with due deference to human happiness and welfare. This underlines the importance of beta humans also having the equivalent of a 'Jerusalem' to bind all people into their common mission. Beta humans must elevate the minds of their fellow humans out of standby mode and find methods of upgrade that can guarantee that all of those who participate will yield improvements. Upgrades must be to the visible betterment of all individual human beings rather to macro-economic factors. And for all its flaws, liberal democracy will be essential to achieving this.

To become a beta human is to elevate your mind out of standby mode and to use your kinship with other human beings and your sovereign freedom as an individual to share in the collective endeavour to improving all of human life. By contrast the central control that China has leveraged into improving the lives of hundreds of millions of its citizens requires people to submit into obedience. I witnessed this at one of the attractions that lies just outside Lijiang: the Jade Dragon Snow Mountain. It is the most southerly snowcapped mountain in the Northern Hemisphere, and one of the highest mountains in a range that continues to Tibet and into the Himalayas. The peak stands 5,596 meters and would be beautiful for hiking and skiing were it not for the thin air of the extremely high altitude.

I set off from Lijiang toward the Jade Dragon Snow Mountain with warm feelings about the prospect of enjoying the freedom of the great outdoors – or rather, catching a cable car for most of the way and then climbing to the final peak. The first thing that was surprising, is that I was required to park up at a large visitor center a few kilometers from the mountain, to buy a pass. The car park was full of coaches of Chinese tourists who were each hiring bright red arctic coats and buying individual bottles of Oxygen.

"Do I have to hire the big red coat?" I enquired of the ticket office, who advised me that it was a little bit cold, but not dangerously cold, and so my hoodie was more than sufficient. Any of the Chinese tourists could have made that same enquiry, but they don't. They followed an obedient pack mentality. If others were hiring a red coat then that is simply what was unquestioningly done.

When I reached the foot of the mountain there was another coach park and visitor center, and some Disney-style ticket barriers. Once through the barriers I was loaded onto an airport bus amongst a convention of red arctic coats, and after a ten minute journey up the mountain, ejected into a line to embark onto the cable car. The signage promoted the cable car as "the longest cable car in the world". It isn't - not by a long way - but most are happy to indulge the fiction.

The queueing barriers snaked around and back on themselves several times, and my eye caught that of an American couple in their fifties, both wearing shorts. When I was nineteen I had bought a 1960 Triumph Spitfire sports car that I drove regularly, and whenever another Triumph of the same era drove toward me, we would flash our headlights at each other in mutual acknowledgement. And similarly, each time that the American couple and I passed each other in the snaking line, we shared a nod of acknowledgement at the absurdity of the red arctic coats and the level of submission to official processes that was required just to go up a mountain compared to in the West, where we would be free to climb and explore a multitude of trails entirely under our own volition and at our own risk.

Eventually I reached the peak and disembarked the cable car into a large café and then outside of the café onto a wooden decked platform. The large platform narrowed at one end into a series of paths and stairs which led to the very top peak of the mountain. Which was closed. I expected to find common cause with my fellow tourists in my frustration that there had been no prior warning about the peak being closed, and that we had been incited to visit under false pretenses. But all I found was willing acceptance - and more compliance.

The clouds were also so thick that there was no visibility beyond one hundred yards. But that didn't seem to bother any of the tourists, who stood huddled together all along the path like hundreds of red emperor penguins, using selfie sticks to capture photos of themselves in their red arctic coat with oxygen bottles. You simply couldn't see anything. The wooden-decked mountain path, which included safety barriers to hold on to on both sides, was closed. And you weren't allowed to touch or walk on the mountain or, god forbid, attempt to leave the designated wood-decked paths to walk onto the snow. There really was nothing to do except wait in the vain hope that the fog might lift. Yet all of the tourists were in their element. They didn't care about conquering the mountain. They had no interest in the view that the fog was obscuring. They just wanted a social media photo of themselves wearing a red arctic coat so they could post the photo and geo-tag it as Jade Dragon Snow Mountain. Tick.

After deciding that waiting for the fog to clear was a lost cause, and after posing with lots of Chinese tourists who wanted a souvenir photo with the strange European who had ascended the mountain in a pair of jeans and a hoodie, I jumped onto another bus that travelled to the nearby Lanyue Lake, a curiously blue coloured man-made lake with a good view of the mountains. Layue Lake is nice enough, but was built solely because a bureaucrat somewhere in the Government decided that the area needed more things for tourists to look at, much like a theme park might built a new ride every year to stay relevant. I spent an hour walking around it and took some photos, and then boarded the bus again.

I flew from Lijiang to Hangzhou in Zhejiang Province, where I had booked to stay for a few days in my own small converted tea house in an old ancient village that had once served the needs of the monks of the seven sacred Buddhist temples nearby, which for centuries had been a popular location for pilgrimage. One of the things that you have the opportunity to see a lot when visiting new places is religious buildings. Britain has its cathedrals and Norman churches. Europe has the great Basilica's of Catholicism. And Asia has its temples. I spent a few days lounging around the tea house and walking amidst the tea plantations near Hangzhou, paying cursory attention to the temples, most of which were modern rebuilds, though there were some ancient rock paintings of Buddha too. The trouble I have with rock and cave paintings is that a few years ago in Sri Lanka I visited the Sigiriya ancient rock fortress. The completely inaccessible fortress was built in 500BC high atop a naturally occurring rock that is two hundred meters high with almost sheer vertical drops on all sides. It became an inaccessible Buddhist monastery for many centuries until the fourteenth Century, and was almost forgotten until spotted by a Major in the British Army in 1831, and then ignored until archaeological work began on a small scale in the 1890's. When the archaeologists explored the many caves atop Sigiriya, they discovered what the monks had been doing up there alone for hundreds of years: filling the walls with over five hundred erotic paintings of naked women with large breasts. And once that you have spent time with those ancient Sri Lankan frescos, ancient Chinese rock paintings of Buddha are just a bit too soft to invoke any real excitement.

The problem that China has when looked at from a Western perspective – and I by no means want to suggest that this is a more valid than a Chinese perspective which may differ greatly – is that on masse, the people do not really know how to enjoy and appreciate things that are natural and beautiful. Not yet anyway. Chinese people like brands because they curate what is beautiful or aesthetically pleasing *for them*. They go through the motions of visiting places not to try to feel an emotional connection with their beauty or history or stories, but because to visit these locations is what is *expected* of one with the means to do so. And they create places to visit and interesting things to see on a 'paint by numbers' basis such that historical sites and man-made beautiful settings feel entirely synthetic and derivative. Almost nothing that is old is original. And almost nothing that is beautiful is real. And nobody knows any better – or really cares.

This kind of group behaviour is inevitable in a society where only three decades ago the entire economy was centrally planned, mandated jobs were allocated and one's entire life was predetermined and ordered. Now Chinese people find themselves with more freedom and money, and they're still working out exactly what to do with it. It is beyond doubt that Chinese citizens are substantially better off than they once were. But this has not been garnered by an unspoken collective endeavour. They are the passive subjects of centrally mandated changes that have improved their lives, rather than being the architects of them. China shows that it is possible to create human betterment from the upgrade of a country's entire 'operating system' – but the successful Chinese experiment has not been humanistic.

Beta humans exist in harmony with each other not because it is mandated, but because that is the right and humanistic thing to do. They create art and music and beauty because those things are the ultimate expression of our existence as a human beings. But a nation cannot achieve these things within a rigid societal structure which achieves social conformity by prescribing the best way to live one's life whilst also discouraging imagination or rebellion. And one can't help but observe a lack of imagination when observing Chinese tourists 'ticking off' experiences at which they have been present for but have had no emotional connection with other than taking a photo for social media. Tick.

And with that thought, I caught my flight to Shanghai.

Whilst Beijing is the heart of Government, Shanghai is the financial powerhouse of China with ambitions to rival the primacy of New York and London as the facilitator and financier of global trade. Shanghai is a city that is increasingly succeeding in this ambition as China extends its lead as the industrial powerhouse of the world. It is all too easy for those in the West to sneer at this, because of its basis in exceptionally cheap labour working in sometimes questionable conditions. Yet when the hymn Jerusalem was first printed as a poem in 1808, lines such as "and was Jerusalem builded here…among those dark satanic mills" were composed to strike a deliberate contrast between the 'Heaven' briefly created in England by a visit by Jesus and the "dark Satanic Mills" of the industrial revolution of England at that time, which included atrocious working conditions which very often caused deformity and disease and hastened death amongst the workers who toiled for a pittance, many of whom were children. It is all too easy to condemn such practices today, but the path to modernity is a difficult one in which decisions are taken about how much tolerance can be mustered for intolerable practices that will lead to a better future.

Should the eight hundred million Chinese who have been lifted out of poverty, or the 1.3 billion Chinese who since 2011 also now enjoy free Universal Healthcare, be condemned back to the poverty and simplicity of their agrarian villages, because the well-trodden path to their life-enhancing modernity includes too many hardships? It's a question that is too big to answer, and certainly not one that can be easily answered in Shanghai.

Much like the London of the early 1800's was teeming with the grand households of the 'new money' industrialists who kept their factories and "satanic mills" at arms-length in the Midlands and the North, Shanghai is where the newly-minted industrialists and financiers of China come to play. I resolved myself to experience the finer side of the vast city by checking into a nice hotel and booking dinner by a Michelin-starred chef with an excellent view of the Shanghai Tower, World Financial Center and Oriental Pearl.

Since my mid-twenties I have long enthused that there is no greater indulgence in life than to submit yourself into the authority of a Michelin starred chef and defer to the expertise of his sommelier for a multi-course tasting menu complete with matching wine flights. In the hands of a good chef, food can take you to places that are sensual and surprising and gratifying beyond all of the usual limitations of human pleasure. Shanghai has a growing contingent of Michelin star restaurants to serve its successful and wealthy - or those like me who will eat nothing but $1 noodles for a fortnight to save up for

164

one amazing Michelin starred meal - and I was curious to discover whether this type of food, which breaks the conventional rules and challenges expectations, would be one of the ways that Shanghai's elite are breaking away from conformity. I also wanted to test my theory that with greater personal wealth, Chinese people were departing from the group-think that I had observed atop the Jade Dragon Snow Mountain, and being more demanding about wanting the best of everything that is available, and demanding it in a way that is completely personalized for the individual, not for the masses. In short, I wanted to know if food was giving China's elite a greater appetite for the pleasures of individualism.

What I found was the opposite of submitting one's self in deference to the finely-honed expertise of a chef, because I was presented with a menu of seemingly infinite variations of tasting menus of different lengths and variety. The dishes included a few novel flairs - a giant crab leg served in a jar in which smoke was trapped, a bit of foam here, a deconstructed something else there – but the overall sense was that I was taking part in a transaction, not an experience, and that the food was designed first-and-foremost so that it could be photographed and posted onto social media. Tick.

As I salved myself with some very excellent wine, I contemplated how the middle class Chinese tourists that I had encountered in their masses throughout my trip had seemed determined to outsource and submit responsibility for their enjoyment and amusement to formal tours and itineraries, and so they missed out on the opportunity to make choices that would give them a more personal, individual and ultimately special experience. But conversely, when it came to very expensive food, the Chinese elite were demanding menus that gave them lots of personalized choices to make for themselves at precisely the moment where it would be infinitely more advisable and enjoyable to submit responsibility for their enjoyment to the Michelin-starred chef, for whose expertise and experience they were actually paying. But rather than dwell on these contrarian tendencies, I ordered a good dessert wine and delved into the pudding menu.

The next evening I descended some stairs to below street level and bought my ticket for the Bund Sightseeing Tunnel, a 646 metre tunnel that has been converted into a multimedia light and sound show. I boarded the train-style glass carriage and stood for the five minutes that it takes to cross underneath the river whilst observing the complex lightshow that was projected onto the walls of the tunnel from every possible angle. The Sightseeing Tunnel is the most wonderful folly. It has no practical purpose other than to entertain and amuse. In 1814 Marc Brunel, son of the famous engineer Isambard Kingdom Brunel, proposed a 396 meter-long tunnel in London that became the first tunnel in history to be constructed successfully under a navigable river. When it opened in 1843 connecting Rotherhithe to Wapping, it quickly became a major tourist attraction, attracting over two million tourists a year, which equates it in popularity, as a proportion of population choosing to visit, with the modern day Disneyland in Florida. Travel writers of the day declared that "nobody visits London without visiting the tunnel", though by 1855 visitors started reporting that the tunnel was rife with stalls telling tat, theft, prostitution and illicit sex and other crimes.

China by contrast has historically had a low level of crime. Not so long ago, people were taught that assets belonged to everybody, and so there wasn't much that people valued enough to steal given the harsh punishments that theft attracted. But for every decade since the Deng reforms, as the economy has shifted further toward Capitalism, China has experienced a marked increase in rates of crime including drugs, prostitution, murder and kidnapping – albeit from a very low initial base level by global standards. China may have upgraded its operating system to define the model for economic growth at the start of the Twenty First Century, but it shows no sign that it's unique 'Socialist Market Economy' is creating a country where crime and anti-social behaviors are any less pervasive than they are in the West. The more capitalist China becomes, the more that crime grows in prominence in what was previously a relatively crime-free society.

I thought of this as I collected my tickets to the observation deck of The Shanghai Tower, which is the world's second tallest building after the Burj Kalifa in Dubai. It may have been beaten to the title of the world's tallest building, but the Tower can still boast the world's fastest elevators and the world's highest observation deck. Shanghai is not building great swathes of skyscrapers – though don't get me wrong there are plenty - but for as far as the eye can see, there are buildings of all shapes and sizes and eras. And it contributes to the overall sense that you get of Shanghai, which is that it doesn't care too much about trying to persuade you that it is going to become one of the financial centres of the world by building great 'future city' cathedrals of capitalism. Shanghai is too busy *becoming* a great financial centre of the world.

China now specialises in 'debt-trap diplomacy', whereby it makes a country economically dependent on its investment and then starts to demand control. In 2017 Sri Lanka was forced to give its largest port, Hambantota, to China after its debts to Chinese companies spiralled out of control. And the 'Belt and Road Initiative' is an unprecedented and audacious plan to extend Chinese influence by recreating the Silk Road trade route for the twenty first century.

The Belt and Road Initiative will be the biggest infrastructure project in human history, and will include Shanghai financiers underwriting construction projects in more than sixty countries across Asia, Africa and Europe at a cost of more than $8 trillion. It will include roads in Kazakhstan, ports in Sri Lanka, industrial parks in Belarus, energy projects in central Asia and railways in Iran and East Africa. It is so titanic that it represents one of the biggest 'upgrades' that the world has ever seen. It is the kind of infrastructure development that will define the first beta humans by bringing more human contact and prosperity to hundreds of millions of people in the world. There are already hundreds of millions of Chinese living lives of abundant new opportunities and pleasures that their parents could never have dared to dream of. And now China is exporting this same model to the wider world too.

Yet increasingly Chinese people are not free citizens but subjects of the state. By the end 2020 China's Communist Party will have completed the fully-functional roll out of a 'social credit' system that will rank all 1.4 billion Chinese citizens on their behaviour. Completing community service and buying Chinese products will improve your social standing. Fraud, tax evasion, smoking in no-smoking areas and buying items that the Government disapproves of such as alcohol or video games, will drop your ranking.

A network of 600 million AI-powered surveillance cameras will enforce the system using facial recognition, body scanning and geo-tracking technology, as well as tracking the online behaviour of every single citizen. It will then give each citizen a 'real time' score out of 800. 'Top rated' citizens get VIP treatment at airports, discounted loans, waived deposits on hotel and car rentals and fast-tracking to elite Universities. 'Low rated' citizens will be barred from the best jobs, cut off from the Internet and blocked from sending their children to the best schools.

Trials of the implementation have seen journalists banned from buying property or booking flights for indiscretions as seemingly minor as sending Tweets that the Government deemed undesirable, which suggests that the one-party state might use the social credit system to enforce an unprecedented level of conformity to centrally-mandated behaviours. An official outline of the system claims that it will "allow the trustworthy to roam freely under heaven while making it hard for the discredited to take a single step".

Even if we allow for discrepancies in translation, the invoking of "heaven" feels particularly ironic in the context of considering what China's colossal progress can teach beta humans. The Chinese government wholly believes that it is upgrading the Chinese operating system using technologies that will help to create a 'Jerusalem' equivalent of 'heaven on earth' for all of its citizens. But will they be beta humans? No.

The concept of beta humans being improvers, builders and upgraders is derived from the notion that the inherent limitations of the internal software of human beings means that we can only improve ourselves so much as individuals, and therefore to attain the next stage of our evolution and become 'beta' humans we must work together to improve our collective existence.

By upgrading the operating systems of the world in which we must exist, beta humans seek not to replace our internal software, but to augment it in ways that allow all humans to escape the limitations of our individual internal software and access betterment.

Yet in its social credit system, the Chinese government is implementing an operating system in which the internal software of sovereign individuals becomes redundant. China's new operating system will not serve, augment or elevate humans, but make them servants to it. And so whilst the scale of China's ambition offers much for beta humans to learn from, the method by which it has sought to upgrade its operating systems should serve as more of a cautionary tale.

And with that thought, I boarded my flight, to Russia.

RUSSIA

My maternal grandmother was born in Patna in India in 1919 and in late 1930's married my Glaswegian grandfather who was serving in the British army. They lived in Hong Kong and Singapore for more than two decades before returning to the deprivation of 1960's Glasgow with four children. At that same time my father lived with his parents and three brothers in a single room of a Glasgow tenement building with no indoor water. It was in Glasgow that my father met my mother, and how I find myself today with genetics that are one-quarter Indian and three-quarters Glaswegian.

Eventually a Doctor told my grandfather that years of chain smoking and Glasgow pollution had obliterated his lungs so badly that he must retreat to cleaner air, and so my grandparents moved to a small post-industrial market town in the midlands of the UK that was remarkable only for being entirely unremarkable.

I am told by my mother that when they first arrived in the town, the air always smelled and tasted of beer thanks to a Joules brewery at the heart of the town. I often wonder if the lingering scent of beer was what persuaded my grandfather to settle in the town when he weighed up the alternatives to Glasgow, though the thought processes of my grandparents on this matter are a mystery, because they are the same people who chose the grinding life of cold and rainy Glasgow over living the relative high life in Hong Kong and Singapore.

It was the 1970's when my grandparents first arrived in the midlands of Britain. At that time casual racism was engrained and endemic. My grandmother was the only non-white face in town and would regularly face racial taunts, shouts and abuse in the streets, as well as more subtle forms of discrimination. When I first introduced one of my young school friends to my grandmother he said to me afterward, with no hint humour: "you didn't tell me that your gran was a paki!!" – which was a derogatory name for Indians and Pakistanis at that time.

And how did my grandmother respond to these times? She would never go out without her hair and makeup being immaculate. She attended church three times a week. She volunteered every week at the local Community Centre. She attended bingo nights and looked after her group of friends. She cooked big meals for her family and friends and pushed her children to succeed, with one joining the British Army. I can say with confidence that not once did my grandmother ever expect the world to yield to her. And she respected every part of her adopted country as she embraced and pursued her ambition not just to be a part of it, but to be a fine and upstanding member of the community that she loved, despite its prejudices to her.

The most powerful tool that my grandmother had was a world apart from the modern vogue for Twitter-mobs, protests and universal proclamations of 'offence'. Her values were a very simple refusal to be a willing recipient of any prejudice. She did not judge those with prejudices, and neither did she allow herself to be influenced or impacted by them: she simply continued to be 'out and proud' as a good human being. To face down adversity with unrelenting stoicism and to triumph. To face hatred but not give way to hating. To hold on when there is nothing to hold on to. To care for and look after others despite any prejudices that they hold toward you. These were the simple values that she, possibly unwittingly subscribed to and lived by, and her children and grandchildren were better for it.

These values from a woman born in 1919 are in many ways also what would define the a modern beta human. By definition a beta human accepts that the greatest opportunity for individual betterment is to upgrade and improve everything around us – the entire operating system – and to use technologies and innovations to leverage that operating system to confer upon each human a level of betterment that they could never achieve by relying solely on their own internal software. And so it follows that to fully benefit from these upgrades, beta humans must, by definition, sacrifice a small element of their individual sovereignty into that operating system in order to achieve the necessary interconnectivity and interdependence with it.

But this poses an important question for beta humans, which is how to reconcile the necessary sacrifice of a portion of individual sovereignty without compromising on the humanist values which are self-evident in their importance? Because humans cannot collectively redefine the purpose of the relatively short time that we will spend as sentient beings if that time is spent entirety subservient to 'operating systems'.

There is one country in the world that has been staunch in upholding its values as it has modernised. So it is a good case for beta humans to study. It is Russia.

I had worked on a few filming projects in Russia over the years, and an in-the-know friend had recommended that if I ever found myself in Moscow again, I should visit the rooftop bar atop the Ritz-Carlton hotel, which looks directly out onto Red Square and the Kremlin. I'm not usually enamoured by the prospect of fashionable noisy bars, especially those types of bars that are frequented by extraordinarily well-presented 'beautiful' people. More than once I have wondered into these bars in Chelsea, only to be taken aback by the vacuity of a crowd with no remarkable talents or achievements aside from spending their parents cash.

A few days before arriving in Moscow I had extended the time that I was prepared to walk from my front door in London to a local pub from five minutes to a whole ten minutes. And as a result of this radial largesse, I had found myself in a delightfully understated Wapping pub called Turner's Old Star. Dating back to 1830 – which is positively 'modern' for a London pub – the Old Star is one of the last-remaining traditional East End pubs in London. It's the kind of pub where you can be assured of warm hospitality, friendly atmosphere and great beers. And it's also a pub with a good story.

Immortalised in film by Director Mike Leigh, former child prodigy Joseph Turner was the most highly-regarded artist of his time. After first selling paintings from the window of his father's barber shop, Turner began his formal training at the Royal Academy aged 14, and aged 24 he was elected as an Associate Member of the Royal Academy – the world's most prestigious institution for art and artists. Turner amassed critical acclaim and considerable wealth, and was entertained constantly by the Lords and Ladies of high society.

But Turner also had a non-conformist rebellious streak to his personality. He was exceptionally secretive and rumoured to have kept several mistresses who bore him many illegitimate children. Upon his death, copious quantities of erotic drawings were discovered amongst his personal affects, supposedly drawn during his many days of drunken debauchery in the pubs of Wapping.

In 1833 Turner met Sophia Booth, who would remain his mistress until his death in 1851. When Turner inherited two cottages in Wapping, he converted them into a pub 'The Old Star' and installed Sophia as the landlady. Then, to maintain his secrecy during their life together at The Old Star, Turner adopted Sophia's surname. The locals who frequented The Old Star – mostly dock workers - came to know the man who occasionally appeared behind the bar as 'Puggy Booth' because of his short height and tubby physique. What they did not know is that the man who was serving them beer was in fact one of the most revered and influential and successful artists in all of British history. And that seems an appropriate confirmation of the adage that you should never judge a book by its cover.

That adage is also pertinent when it comes to Russia, where thankfully the rooftop bar at the Ritz-Carlton was not frequented Chelsea-types, but by a relatively relaxed crowd from all over the world who were talking enthusiastically in small groups and occasionally pausing to breathe-in the view across Red Square toward the magnificent and iconic St Basil's Cathedral.

Bars in Russia are free to open all night if that is the will of their customers, and so it was that at nearly three in the morning I was drinking a cold beer in a comfy chair, feeling like the most free man in the entire world.

And it also helps that Russians are exceedingly good hosts. I'd had a very long day of being shown the sights of Moscow in between attending meetings that had been scheduled for me during my trip. When alone in Moscow I had always used Uber to get around, but my Russian host didn't have the requisite patience that's needed when waiting for an Uber to arrive, and so in between each meeting, he had simply flagged down a passing car, and paid the driver a few Roubles to take us to wherever we wanted or needed to go.

At first this was disconcerting. Moscow is packed full of modern cars like any other major city, but by chance, or perhaps by self-selection, one of the cars that we flagged down happened to be a Lada Riva from the Soviet Era. It must have been one of only a handful of such cars left on the roads in all of Moscow, and the driver had been smoking so consistently that the windows had turned an oblique yellow. The passenger door was also so severely dented that it was stuck permanently closed. But the driver, who was not a taxi driver and presumably was driving with the purpose of actually going somewhere before we had flagged him down, was happy to drive us, and once that he discovered that I was British, continually urged my Russian host to point out the many sights of interest.

One of those sights was the Cathedral of Christ the Savior, which became notorious in the West in February 2012 when three young members of the band-come-protest-group Pussy Riot burst into the church in their trademark coloured clothes and knitted balaclavas, and performed an obscenity-laced song called Punk Prayer, which attacked the Orthodox church's support for Vladimir Putin. They were arrested and held without bail until July 2012, when they were sentenced to two years in prison each for "hooliganism motivated by religious hatred". One was released early in October, and the other two in December 2014 after tough jail time. As a result of the Christ the Saviour protest, the feminist band morphed into an international cause celebre that divided Russia and attracted the attention of celebrities and human rights groups. For a time their distinctive coloured balaclavas became a widely-recognised symbol and the name 'Pussy Riot' is now synonymous worldwide as a symbol of protest against what some term the 'regime' of Vladimir Putin.

Throughout the international reporting of the protest and subsequent arrests and imprisonment, there was a key aspect of the Christ the Saviour story that was notable by its absence. The lofty cathedral, with its famous gilded golden domes and crisp white marble elevations, was consecrated in 1883, the day before Alexander III was crowned, and its interior was decorated by some of the finest artists of the day. But less than fifty years later the 1917 Russian revolution mandated atheism as the 'official' state 'religion' of the Soviet Union and the subsequent 1921–1928 anti-religious campaign saw the systematic destruction of most churches. Christ the Saviour did not escape the destruction. In 1930 the gold domes were melted down to recover 20 tons of gold, and in 1931 the entire Cathedral was dynamited. It took more than a year to clear the debris from the site. Then in 1958 the site - a place of great spiritual and emotional importance for observant Russians - was transformed into the world's largest heated open air swimming pool.

It wasn't until 1990 that the Russian Orthodox Church received permission to rebuild the cathedral, and one million Muscovites (from a population of nine million) donated funds to rebuild what was initially intended as a replica, but in reality included major design changes and modern innovations. In 1994 the outdoor swimming pool was demolished, and the 'new' Cathedral was opened in August 2000, 69 years after it was first destroyed. It's hard to imagine a project today that could attract donations from one-in-nine people in a city. In cities people increasingly live piled and packed-in on top of one another in apartments, and yet they have such a great assortment of choices enabling them to tread such a personalised path through their life that it is extremely rare for all of the paths of all of the people to converge at the same time so as to bring them together in support of an important national project.

The 'back story' of Christ the Saviour was notably absent in Western reporting of the Pussy Riot protest in 2012. Its absence suffocated the opportunity for a better international comprehension and understanding of the events. By reducing the story to the bare bones of a Sampson-versus-Goliath act of rebellion, news outlets reduced their readers to an ignorant blindness equivalent that of the drinkers who berated the ugly and seemingly 'talentless' Puggy Booth in The Old Star.

One might argue that this was because the back-story didn't support the simplified narrative of a small protest group standing up to one of the most powerful men in the world? Who knows really. But what is clear is that Christ the Saviour isn't just any old cathedral – it is a national symbol of Russians regaining their religious freedom after a terrible period of history during which the state deprived them of their freedom to worship, but through which many thousands secretly kept the faith.

I'm not suggesting that Pussy Riot were wrong in their protest. The freedom to instigate peaceful protest and rebellion against a government that you disagree with is a cornerstone of all freedom. But the back story of Christ the Savior makes it easier to understand the condemnation of the protest, because it could easily be mis-perceived as an affront to a religious freedom that had arisen from the dynamited rubble of the great hardships, cruelties and religious oppression that had been imposed by the former Communist regime.

This over-simplification of news stories involving Russia is a preoccupation of Western media and politicians who often fail in their comprehension of the nuances. Russians are overwhelmingly proud people who are wedded to the facts of a practical reality and who give little indulgence to abstract concepts. Place an English-speaking Russian in a British pub, and he will engage the locals in conversations and anecdotes and dour humour; and the locals will be shocked by the similarities in their values and outlook. Russians are also wholly aware that the political and economic situation in their country could be better. But as with so many things that are shaped by history, they also know

- because for many it is within living memory - that things could be an awful lot worse than they are.

Russians also take light offence at how the West characterises an entire nation of 144 million people. And they carry a near-disbelief about how popular British and American history so often dilutes or ignores the role and sacrifices of the Russian people in liberating Europe from Hitler. Could the Allies have defeated the Nazis without the huge Russian contribution? The answer is, quite simply, no.

Of course, the world paid a huge price for Russian support in ending World War II. Winston Churchill was in the room at the 1945 Yalta Conference to plan Europe's post war reorganization, but despite the victory rhetoric, by the end of the war Britain was crippled and bankrupt. It was Roosevelt and Stalin who decided how to carve up Europe. And as we all know, much of Eastern Europe was ceded into the USSR, where it remained until the fall of communism in 1989.

On one of my trips to the beautiful and enthralling city of St Petersburg, I once enjoyed a journey to the airport with a local taxi driver who spoke excellent English, and being Russian, was eager to give good hospitality by engaging me in conversation. As we preceded to drive through a fairly nondescript suburb on the way to the airport, he pointed out without a flicker of emotion that we were driving over a site where the Nazis had concentrated their firepower as they shelled Russian soldiers in their failed advance toward St Petersburg. It was also the grave of the many thousands of Russian soldiers who buried where they fell in the chaos of war.

The Siege of Leningrad, as St Petersburg was briefly known, lasted for 29 months from September 1941. By Hitler's order, German troops constantly shelled and bombed the city and systematically isolated it from any supplies, causing the death of more than one million civilians in three years. A secret Nazi document from 23 September 1941 implied an intended genocide of the population of St Petersburg in its instruction that "the Fuhrer is determined to eliminate the city of Petersburg from the face of the earth". And so it follows that modern Russians favour having a leader who is strong enough to ensure that they never have to fend off a foreign power ever again – and who asserts what they regard as their rightful status on the global stage.

Whilst the West regularly disparages and, to use street slang, "disrespects" Russia, leaders like Vladimir Putin can be relied upon by Russians to consistently keep the world reminded of how the strength of their country was crucial in shaping the modern world as we know it, which is why he was elected to a fourth term in 2018 with over seventy seven percent of the popular vote. When Russians vote in their droves for Putin, they aren't necessarily drinking the cool aid of Russia being a 'superpower'. They know that their economy is completely dwarfed by the USA and China. But there is also a sense that Russia deserves better recognition on the global stage – and it is Putin who can deliver.

And so whenever I have been in Russia, what I have always encountered is that as well as being welcoming and hospitable, the people also resolve themselves to a kind of 'heroic stoicism', a 'blitz spirit' that no matter what happens in global geopolitics, they will simply get on with things. You get the sense that without it being spoken, Russians collectively know that most global politics can be reduced to no more than different nations puffing themselves up for each other like jocks on a football field. And so the Russians send out their biggest global player to jostle with the big boys and to keep some Russian skin in the game, but mostly, they then just leave him to it whilst they get on with their own lives, which are more important than geopolitics.

It would be easy to suggest the 'blitz spirit' that seems to bind all Russians arises from the fact that all young men must complete one year of compulsory military service. But actually it is the women of Russia who exemplify the heroic stoicism most of all. I became acutely aware of this during a trip to Moscow in 2016. I attended a meeting with a colleague, a slow-moving fellow Brit in his fifties who was portly-verging-on-rotund. We had just finished a meeting and as we walked along the street, the sound of gunshots repeatedly rang out, and just ahead of us we spotted a young man who was seemingly firing a handgun in rage. He wasn't actually shooting at anyone, he was simply shooting the gun at the ground and into the sky outside an office building, but the handful of people who had been nearby were now all running for cover.

What to do in this situation is not something that arrives as a quick decision in the heat of the moment. After a startled pause, my colleague and I realised that we were now the only targets left in the street, and so we turned on our heels and ran for cover. My abiding memory is of running as fast as I could, trying to remember whether it is better to run in a straight line or to zig zag to avoid gun shots, and being surprised that my older, portly colleague was running right along-side me at the same pace. "How is he managing to keep up?" I wondered as we sought safety in a nearby office.

That evening we regaled the story to our Russian-born host, a thirty-something mother of two who had married a Brit. She was unmoved by our experience, and suggested that it was likely someone playing an unfunny practical joke rather than anything dangerous. "But how would anyone know if it was real?" I asked her. "Men do silly things sometimes…he was probably trying to impress a girl or something" she said.

Of course this collective Russian stoicism can occasionally be shaken. In 2014 when EU sanctions over Putin's occupation of Crimea meant that the country's supply of European wine and cheese were cut off, the sense of loss was palpable amongst middle class Russians because, contrary to stereotypes, it is wine, not vodka, that Russians increasingly prefer to imbibe.

Since December 1991 Russia has prevailed on the difficult path of upgrading and modernising its operating system without making itself entirely dependent on the interconnected operating systems of globalisation, not least because Russia is rich in natural resources and is a net exporter of oil. This has meant that Russia has been able to 'upgrade' without having to compromise much of the sovereignty of individual Russians, which should interest beta humans. That is not to say that Russia's commercial borders are not open with the world. I once spent a cold December morning deep in the suburbs nearly two hours outside the centre of Moscow, attending the opening of a local supermarket – the first to open in the area. The temperature was many degrees south of zero, but for more than one hour before the doors opened, the indomitable babushkas - the Russian matriarchs who sit at the head of Russian families - patiently lined up outside without issue or complaint. This strength of Russian women should be classified by UNESCO as a world intangible heritage, especially because Russians have a deep cultural respect for strong women. It was a Soviet journalist, not the British, who coined the moniker 'Iron Lady' for Margaret Thatcher. It was intended as an insult, but by the time that Thatcher left office in 1990, for Russians it had become a term of affection, or at least grudging respect, for her strength.

Seeing the babushkas queue up in the cold for a supermarket opening had been like my own micro-version of the opening of the first McDonalds in the Soviet Union in 1990, when 1,000 Russians were expected to visit, but actually 30,000 showed up and dutifully queued patiently in the freezing cold to get their first taste of the American fast food. And after my late night of drinking in the bar overlooking Red Square, I was glad that McDonalds had long since become a ubiquitous sight in Moscow as I craved some complex carbohydrates. I recalled that on a previous occasion I had spotted a McDonalds at the exit to one of the subways that had taken me underneath the road and into Red Square, and decided that I would see if I could salve my hangover with an Egg McMuffin.

Red Square is one of those places that attracts a lot of tourists who don't really know what to do once that they get there. I've realised that a similar thing happens to first time visitors to Paris when they encounter the Eiffel Tower: they go to the tower, take some photos and might even ascend to the top of it. It is so familiar and so iconic to them that, surely, they must 'do something' to interact with it when they visit. They of course quickly learn that the Eiffel Tower is simply the backdrop to the joy de vivre of Paris. One can indulge in everything that Paris has to offer, get lost in its gastronomy, nourish the coffee, satiate yourself in the patisserie – and the Eiffel Tower will be quietly watching over you as an enduring symbol of the freedom to enjoy life and not to take it too seriously.

My own first experience of Red Square was very late at night after arriving on an earlier flight but getting lost in an unlicensed taxi. I admit I had often been amused at the naivety of foolhardy tourists who arrive somewhere in the world and then lose their shirt by catching an unlicensed taxi from the airport. The logical calculus of tired and jet lagged tourists as they arrive at an airport and accept one of these rides is that it cannot possibly be an unauthorised taxi, because the authorities wouldn't allow such exploits to be so visible. Except they often do. Unlicensed taxi operators prey on this, and can be extremely cynical in their ploys to catch out

197

tourists. And for some reason on my first trip to Moscow, which was to do some filming, the cameraman that I was working with and I ended up in an unlicensed taxi going to nowhere. I am always particular about finding an official taxi rank and then insisting that a taxi turns on its meter, but on this occasion, the fraudulent taxis had created a line of the same model of cars in the same colour in a drop off area, which in my jet lagged delirium looked legitimate.

And so as the bitterly cold darkness of the winter night set in, and as my colleague and I both awoke from a nap in the back of the taxi, reasonably expecting to be in central Moscow, it became clear that far from fighting our way along the congested Moscow roads, we had actually driven out of the city and left the highway to travel into the unlit countryside. My colleague turned on the data connection on his phone, and as text messages pinged in to warn him how expensive that was going to be, we checked our location on Google maps and realised our jeopardy.

When you hear about unlicensed taxis, it's usually a story about an elderly couple getting grossly overcharged for a journey. But just occasionally you hear about someone being taken away never to be seen again. And in the deserted cold wastelands outside Moscow, nobody would hear a couple of gunshots. And nobody would be driving by to see any bodies being buried. I don't wear an expensive watch or jewellery, and my smartphone was not worth murdering me for. But my colleague and I were acutely aware that we had a lot of expensive camera equipment in the trunk of the car, as the driver became jittery and nervous and started to drive even faster and erratically.

The power of hindsight always brings clarity, but much like when you encounter a man shooting in the street, when you're in the moment of potential danger, your mind becomes engaged in trying to assess whether that danger is real or perceived. It would be difficult for two British men to enquire of the driver if he intended to imminently murder us both, because if we were wrong, it could be socially awkward, not to mention

199

impolite. It also seemed discourteous to make the driver pull over so that we could mount an offensive attack, especially as we'd need the driver to drive us back again if it turned out that he did not have a gun. Eventually we did what the British do best. We apologised. And politely asked where he was going.

It turned out that the driver had entered the wrong address into his GPS, and had unquestioningly followed it even as it had directed him out of town and into the fields. We were now ninety minutes from the airport, which we would need to drive back to and then drive past to head into central Moscow – a theoretical journey of an additional hour if the traffic is good, but in practical reality many hours in Moscow congestion.

And so after many hours of driving and not being murdered, I checked in to my hotel and decided that I was going to at least manage to see Red Square and take a photo with St Basils Cathedral before going to bed. It was midnight and it took me a while to navigate the tunnels that led under the six-lane road and into Red

Square. I was conscious not to accidentally wander into Moscow's exquisitely-adorned but bafflingly warren-like subway system, but eventually I emerged into Red Square, which at this time of the night contained only a few revellers and tourists. Around the edges and in the shadows of Red Square seemed to be a place where, without wanting to be indecorous, a great number of homosexual men were cruising to meet other men. As I walked past I attracted a lot of smiles, and I smiled back, partly to be polite, but mostly because I was amused that at this symbolic heart of a notoriously anti-gay country was a hotbed of prospective homosexual encounters. Societies can be pious or authoritarian or discriminatory, but ultimately people will be true to their natural inclination! I took my photo with St Basil's Cathedral, remarked upon Lenin's tomb which was closed for refurbishment and took a stroll across a nearby bridge to get a good look at the well-lit walls of the Kremlin from where it lined the banks of the Moskva River. And I couldn't help feeling that were it not for a series of tipping points in history, none of which were inevitable, from the fall of Communism to the breakup of the Soviet Union, for a British person to walk around Red Square late at night to no purpose other than my own amusement would not have been possible at all.

On that first trip to Moscow I had found the endlessness of the Communist tower blocks that emanate out from the city centre for mile upon mile, and the roadside power stations, to all be a little grey and oppressive. Even the grand stone buildings of central Moscow seemed dark and utilitarian. But by the time I made my subsequent visits, aided by a local host, I discovered that what lies behind these utilitarian facades can often be delightfully surprising. Being from a mildly-depressed post-industrial small town in the centre of Britain, I have a typically working-class taste for hearty carbohydrate-rich foods. They are a part-and-parcel of working class life, as engrained in my psyche as never leaving food on your plate and taking your coat off indoors so that you "feel the benefit" once that you step back outside. And so I was very pleased the day that I discovered Georgian food, which beautifully fuses an interplay of culinary ideas carried along the Silk Road Trade route by merchants and travellers, and makes extensive use of breads, cheeses, meat and spicy sauces.

Being Russian, my hosts took their hospitality role very seriously, and so once that they uncovered my liking of Georgian food, insisted on taking me to their favourite Georgian restaurant. And so it was that I found myself heading from my hotel past Christ the Saviour Cathedral into streets that I had not visited before. The streets were lined with stone-fronted buildings, but very few yielded the secret of what lay within. Suddenly we arrived at the door of a building that I could quite easily have walked past without ever venturing that there was anything of interest inside. Yet as I stepped in, I was aghast to find a huge restaurant that had been exquisitely decorated and was filled with at least one hundred people enjoying an evening meal. The Georgian food they served was completely outstanding.

And that restaurant is a good metaphor for Russia. That what you see on the surface is rarely the same as what you experience within. And for that reason it can be hard for someone whose experience is almost entirely of Western culture to get to grips with it. But if you allow yourself to go with the flow, you discover a society that consistently makes use of common sense.

I thought about this as I landed in beautiful St Petersburg. Far away from the nucleus of Russian power that is Moscow. Its Baroque and neoclassical buildings mean that St Petersburg looks and feels much more like a European city, and it is quite rightly regarded as the cultural capital of Russia.

St Petersburg was Founded by Peter The Great in 1703, who made it the capital city from 1732 to 1918. It offers another fascinating case study for beta humans. Determined to 'upgrade' Russia, Peter the Great wanted a port that was on the Baltic Sea so that Imperial Russia could trade more with Europe. He also wanted to modernise the country with a new European-style city that would be close to the heart of Europe and which could impress with palaces to rival Versailles. Much like Dubai has risen from the sands as a hugely ambitious 'future city', St Petersburg rose entirely from the marshes as part of a colossal ambition to create a new city that would bring betterment to its citizens.

Today the historic centre of St Petersburg is a UNESCO World Heritage Site thanks in part to a lucky quirk of history. Most cities are built beside rivers, but there are few cities like St Petersburg where the water is as abundant as brick and stone. Built across the marshlands of the Veva River delta, the city is interlaced with more than one hundred tributaries and canals with a length of over 300 kilometres. There are more than 800 bridges crossing them. And so by accident rather than by design, when the Communists oversaw the wanton and systematic destruction of many fine buildings in Russia to be replaced with Soviet-style concrete tower blocks to "house the people", St Petersburg was able to escape the worst of the destruction, because its marshland foundations and small waterway-intersected islands did not offer a sound foundation for high-rise concrete architecture.

I spent time strolling the famous granite embankments that are home to many of the city's grandest buildings, and paid a long visit to the vast Hermitage Museum. Afterwards, lulled into artlessness by the sense of freedom and the romance of strolling the fine and handsome streets and bridges of the city, I considered whether regardless of how politically aggressive Russia may seem from the outside, it had managed to achieve something important for beta humans in retaining a strong national identity? Had the occasionally obtuse and often contrarian nature of Russia, either by accident or design, created the kind of conditions where beta humans could thrive without surrendering portions of their sovereign freedom into their operating system?

I got my answer later that day when I was arrested and held by the Russian authorities as a possible British spy.

I had been travelling with two colleagues from a film crew. One of those colleagues was a very tall Irishman who regularly enters high-level competitions for

CrossFit, a fitness regimen based on gymnastics, weightlifting, running, rowing and more. His impressive commitment to honing his body and eating well meant that his stature has an undoubtedly 'special forces' military look. The other colleague, who also takes a tough stance on maintaining his fitness, doesn't have quite the same stature, but by coincidence does have the look of the kind of military man who it would be folly to underestimate. Think of one of those former SAS men that you occasionally see in television documentaries, who looks surprisingly slight and lean, but you also know that he could quite easily kill a man with his bare hands before breakfast.

And then there was me, five foot nine with pale skin and my six-pack hidden under a persistent layer of cake and biscuits. I'd like to think that perhaps the Russians assumed I was the swaggering James Bond type and my colleagues were part of my 'crew'. Or, perhaps they assumed I was the brains? M perhaps? Or Q?

I've always thought that the James Bond movie franchise could do a lot more with the Q character. I feel a frustration for my teenage self that it took until I was in my late twenties before smart started to become the new 'sexy' and geek-chic became a thing. When I was at school being the smart geeky kid meant that the librarian always made sure she had quality newspapers stocked for me to read at lunchtime, but there were certainly no other benefits. But the titans of tech have upset that old world order, and now having an ingenious intelligence and a Sherlock-style brilliance is widely desired. And so if I was being regarded as the 'Q' in our alleged British spy cell, then I was happy.

Nobody in Russian security seemed to notice that this "British" spy cell was comprised of one British national, one Irish national and one Spanish national. Maybe that's just how it works in the spying world? Maybe European spooks club together in a kind of secret 'spying club' where they hang out and occasionally go on joint missions to prank the Russian or the American spooks? Our military 'look' wasn't helped by the fact that modern camera equipment looks like sophisticated military equipment and is transported in military-grade boxes. The RED cameras that we had been filming with look ferociously high tech, and between uses they get broken down into various smaller pieces and components that each has to be individually packed. And so when Russian security started opening our cases, what they saw were high tech components that it doesn't take much imagination to believe could be part of a military application. And of course we were also carrying aerial drones for filming, which threw in an entirely new angle of potential espionage.

We did of course have permission from the Russian state to be carrying film cameras and aerial drones. It had taken weeks of form-filling and administration by our local host to get it, yet upon our arrival in Russia, customs had inspected the equipment and waved it through without even asking to see the permission. We hadn't expected to need to show that permission again, and anyway, it soon became clear that permission was not the issue, it was suspicion about our "mission".

To make matters worse, I had a round-the-world flight booked for the next day departing from London Heathrow. A round-the-world ticket lets you travel to as many locations as you wish, on a single ticket, as long as you are always travelling in the same direction that you set off in. So for example, if you set off from London to fly east to Berlin, then you can't then fly to New York unless you continue your journey east around more than half of the globe. And if you miss the first flight in your itinerary, then the remainder of the extremely expensive ticked becomes null and void.

What happened next has always puzzled me. We were being held on the premise of being involved in some form of spying activity. Our flight back to London was due to leave in just a few hours. But Russian security suddenly allowed one of my colleagues to leave, taking all of our hard drives containing all of the footage that we had filmed - including the drone footage - with him. So if we had been using the equipment for spying, then

Russian security had just let the footage freely leave when my colleague boarded a flight back to London.

Next came the interrogations. I knew that during the Cold War the Russians had teams of very beautiful and highly trained agent provocateurs who were experts in seducing men to reveal of all of their secrets. Hoping that not too much had changed since the Cold War, I was separated from my colleague into an interrogation room to explain myself to a small English-speaking man, who translated what I said into Russian for the benefit of a completely disinterested second man who was trying to pick something out of his teeth, and a third man who was scribing the translation using a pencil. "Why use a pencil?" I wondered.

Then the torture started.

After the 'interview' I was taken to sit on a chair in the corner of a messy office, whilst the three men – yes three of them – together typed what the scribe had written in pencil into a computer. The statement was pages long and they typed the kind of slow single-fingered typing that a pensioner does when encountering a QWERTY keyboard for the very first time. The slow speed was excruciating, and it got worse when the statement was printed out several times. It is generally considered a sign of tiresome bureaucracy when forms must be filled out in triplicate. But it turns out, there is actually a whole list of tuples that follow triplicate. Quadruple for four times. Octuple for eight. And undecuple hendecuple for 11. And this is how the torture continued, as the agents printed out more copies of more forms, and proceeded to complete each one by hand, before asking me to sign.

Everything was in Russian so for all I knew I was signing to say that my intentions were to overthrow the Russian Government, but by this stage the torture of the slow bureaucracy was breaking my resolve, as each form was scanned into a laminator and then slowly cut out by hand, one by one. I swear if I had to watch two of the agents watch the third agent cutting out another laminated form, I would have reached for those scissors and gone James Bond on them. Maybe that's what they want? To use tedium to bore you into exposing your spy skills? But unfortunately I didn't have any.

Many hours later, after the three agents had wound up the starter motor on their Internet connection and worked out how to open a browser – which was probably Netscape – to check our credentials, passports were returned and we were free to leave. I got the overwhelming feeling that we were being released because it was the end of their shift, and with my passport in hand again, I gave the English-speaking agent a look that said "You just fucked with me for nearly twelve hours just to create something to do to justify the existence of your own job" but I resisted saying anything. I couldn't take any more torture by tedium, and I'd worked out that if I caught a flight East to Moscow and then waited a few hours, I could then catch a connecting flight to fly back West again over St Petersburg and get to Heathrow two hours before my 10-hour flight to Singapore was due to take off.

There are a great many things to love about Russia, and the Russian people are by far-and-away the greatest thing. But for all of its excellent attributes, even when you're sitting at 3am on a rooftop bar atop the Ritz-Carlton feeling like the most free man in the world, there are latent and menacing state authorities lurking below and waiting to demonstrate the concept of hubris by instigating your fall with a more-than-firm shove between the shoulder blades.

And for that reason, despite the allure of Russia's contrarian tendencies and the enduring strength of its values, the lessons for beta humans are in fact limited.

Perhaps then, there are lessons for beta humans to draw from somewhere that has a culture and society that is so idiosyncratic as to be unlike any other place in the world? Perhaps beta humans can learn from Japan?

JAPAN

For an example of why the beta human philosophy of upgrading entire operating systems to create betterment for all of the humans is a valid endeavour, look no further than the mobile (cell if you are American) phone.   In the mid-1990s my father was an early-adopter of the mobile telephone. He worked as a self-employed welder and pipe fitter, and his office was the front of his white Ford Escort van, which was permanently sooted in welding dust. His mobile phone meant that my father was always available to take calls.

The mobile phone has changed the world for the better far more than many people realise.   In developing nations it has brought banking to the masses and enabled remote communities to start cottage industries that have lifted them out of poverty.   It has helped populations to organise themselves to undermine the control of information by authoritarian regimes. And it gave my father a better chance to provide for his family by always being available when one of his contacts wanted to discuss a new job with him. When my father came home, I would immediately unclasp the phone from his belt and take it outside into the garden, where I would climb onto the roof of the garden shed to play with it. Rarely did I actually make a call or send a message – that was far too expensive. Instead I simply held and played with the keys, amazed to be holding such an amazing piece of technology in my own hands.

The late 1990s marked the beginning of the glory days for the mobile phone. It was a time before Apple and Samsung took over the market with their smartphone duopoly. A time when a phone battery would last for days and the only distraction on offer was to play snake on the tiny green-and-black LCD screen. And it was a time when for me every trip to one of the nearby towns always involved visiting a mobile phone store just to look at the vast variety of designs for handsets that were on offer from a huge variety of technology brands. The Nokia 3210 led a revolution in ergonomics and aesthetics. The Siemens C25 turned the ringtone into a coveted status symbol. The Sony CMD Z5 showed us just how quickly technology could shrink in size, which was then a great indicator of technological progress. The first Motorola Razr established the phone as a fashion accessory. And the then-lauded Blackberry amazed the world with its QWERTY keyboard.

Beta humans are possible only because current humans are fortuitous to find ourselves existing at the moment in history where the chain reaction of accelerating and exponential technological progress has reached an epoch that can completely transform human lives. The speed that technology now changes means that nobody needs to live to an old age to be able to watch the ground breaking technologies of their younger days become redundant. This offers unprecedented opportunities for humanity. And it is the responsibility of beta humans to awaken other humans from their stand-by mode to engage in the collective endeavour of embracing the opportunity to upgrade and improve every single aspect of human existence. Technology will enable many improvements in our individual internal software. But it is in the near-endless opportunities for upgrading the platforms on which we live our lives – the many operating systems of our world – that beta humans could unlock levels of betterment and human experience that go far beyond the imaginations of even our most recent ancestors.

It all started with the motor car. Horses were the main mode of transport for over a thousand years. Then in 1885 Karl Benz invented the first true motor car, and it was just twenty-three years later that Henry Ford unveiled the Model T Ford, the world's first mass-produced car that was affordable for 'the masses'. Only forty-nine years later Jaguar unveiled the E-Type Jaguar, a car that Enzo Ferrari called "the most beautiful car in the world" and which many still regard as the most perfect car ever made. This was followed throughout the 1960's by an explosion of rapid technological improvements in car design, including some very outlandish expositions from Detroit.

That is just 76 years from the first invention of the motorcar technology to the first example of it being widely considered as 'perfected' in the E-Type Jaguar. Yet by modern standards 76 years of technological progress is an eternity: the Internet was only invented in 1990 but has changed the world. The first call from a mobile phone was made in Manhattan in 1973, but by 2007 Apple had released the iPhone and precipitated an abundant technological revolution which means that you probably now carry a supercomputer in your pocket and would be lost without it. In his 2012 book 'Abundance: The Future Is Better Than You Think', Peter H Diamandis calculated that there are approximately $900,000 worth of applications in a typical smartphone. An HD video camera, two-way video conferencing, GPS, libraries of books, your record collection, a flashlight, an EKG, a full video game arcade, a tape recorder, maps, a calculator – not to mention access to the majority of all entertainment that has even been made into television, films, music and books. Before the smartphone, only the super wealthy could buy the equivalent level of utility.

When I was a young teenager, I would never allow my mother to walk my brother and I past a mobile phone store without stopping in to browse the amazing designs and variety of the phones inside, and dreaming that one day we might be able to own our own mobile phone. Yet to look at those phones today is like looking at museum exhibits from a time long-since passed. They were once things of great technology and promise, but the passing of time has rendered them obsolete and devoid of useful utility. They are a reminder of the early promise and excited optimism that people attached to the new technology, which must again be invoked in order to usher in the dawn of beta humans.

I had feelings about rapid obsolescence superseding the early promise of technology when I landed in Tokyo.

It was the kind of feeling that I would get if someone gifted me a Nintendo Game Boy today: I would be very pleased to receive one for nostalgic reasons, but also disappointed that I was experiencing it out of its own time now that it has been so surreptitiously surpassed and out-manoeuvred by a titanic leap forward in techno-innovation that would make it seem entirely diminished relative to the great promise of its heyday.

I had flown the seven hours from Singapore overnight. The trouble with these overnight flights is that you have such a heightened awareness that you must use this time to sleep, that it becomes a near-impossibility. I had a few glasses of red wine before boarding the flight in anticipation of needing to sleep, but I couldn't get comfortable in my seat, and the wine had made me feel dehydrated and irritable rather than making me sleepy.

So I began my Tokyo expedition in a tortuous state of sleep deprivation from which there would be no respite, because I was being met at the airport by my host, a thirty-something scion of a regional publishing dynasty, who had aspirations of persuading me to join him in his family business in Tokyo. He was eager to show me some excellent Japanese hospitality during my 48 hours in Tokyo, before catching the bullet train to travel west for four hours to the very beautiful but mostly-unknown

Fukui Prefecture north of Kyoto, which is the ancient spiritual homeland of both Sushi and Sake.

In most cities in the world it is not uncommon to find two classes of taxi at the airport: the standard no-frills taxi, and the 'premium' taxi, usually a blacked-out Mercedes furnished in comfortable black leather, or in the USA a very large SUV. In Tokyo there is a choice of the traditional and ubiquitous yellow 'Toyota Comfort' taxi, or alternatively a 'premium' black long wheel base 'Toyota Crown Comfort' taxi that is cleaner and air conditioned, with a leather interior, curtains on the windows, a well-dressed driver and clean white crochet doily headrest covers that would greatly impress even the most prim and proper grandmother.

The Toyota Comfort was purpose-built as a taxi, and even though it was first released in 1995 and remained in production until 2017, its styling is straight out of 1980. And this retro design gets accentuated further once that the driver has covered the headrests in pristine white and perfectly-pressed crochet doilies from another era. This was a harbinger of what was to come.

When futuristic cities are portrayed in films or cartoons or in science fiction, they are pristine and new and modern. They have innovative mass transport systems like monorails that fly through the cityscape, and 'neighbourhoods in the sky' thanks to modern skyscrapers filled with homes and offices and leisure facilities. We assume that these cities will keep innovating and building and modernising well into the future, staying ahead of the world as a shining beacon for innovation and modernity. But rarely do we stop to consider what these uber-modern cities will look like if they were to stop building and stop innovating, as in Tokyo. And so when you look out from behind the curtain in the back of a Toyota Crown Comfort and see the Tokyo Monorail trundle past looking rather tired and rusty and propped up on concrete pillars that are stained from age, the effect is much the same as when you encounter an old mobile phone: you can appreciate the glory of its former greatness, but it is hard to escape the reality that the world has since moved away from it.

You expect to see modernity everywhere in Tokyo. For it to be an exposition of technological and economic progress like Shanghai or Dubai or Hong Kong. But there are just 49 buildings and structures that stand taller than 187 metres, and nothing taller than 255 metres, which is just 31% of the height of the Burj Kalifa in Dubai. The entire city feels like a monument to the boom period before what are commonly now known in Japan as the "lost decades" of the 1990's and 2000's following the huge and devastating economic crash of 1989, from which Japan has never really recovered its confidence or international stature.

In the 1960's Japan gained its competitive edge by copying Western products, improving upon them, and then selling them back to the West at cheaper prices. To compensate for Japan's lack of natural resources, Japanese companies focused on developing innovative and efficient manufacturing methods and improving their products, which created a huge competitive advantage in export products such as cars and electronics. By the 1970's Japan's use of assembly-line robots removed human error from the manufacture of cars – a leap forward that shocked the rest of the world's motor industry to its core. It seems strange now to anyone born after 1980, but it was not so long ago that it was entirely normal to expect that your car would break down. It was considered inevitable that such complex machinery as a motor car and combustion engine would often develop faults, until the Japanese showed this conventional wisdom to be wholly wrong.

By the 1980's Japan extended its global domination to the electronics industry, manufacturing the world's consumer products and introducing the world to new innovations such as the VHS recorder and the Sony Walkman, which launched an enduring consumer love affair that continues today with Apple's iPhone. By 1989 Nintendo and Sega owned the entire video game market and Japan was powerhouse of the global electronics industry.

But after decades of stellar economic growth, the crash that followed in 1989 was almost inevitable. It terminally damaged Japan's competitive edge. In 1990 the Japanese stock market plunged by 50% and then kcpt falling until 1992. Unprofitable and debt ridden 'zombie companies' were kept afloat by Government bailouts. As recently as 2004, Tokyo property was only worth 10% of its 1989 peak and the stock market still traded at just a quarter of its high during the boom.

But that is not to say that Japan has nothing to teach and inspire beta humans. There is an implicit unconscious bias in the notion that it will be the younger generations who will bring in the age of beta humans. But if you had to rebuild the world, who would you charge with that responsibility? The inexperienced young? Or the older people who have lived through turmoil and come out of the other end with life experience, albeit slightly weary? Japan has firmly rooted for the latter, and the pressed-and-starched doilies in the Toyota Crown Comfort are a testament to a country where the baton of building the future has not yet been passed to the next generation, but instead remains with a highly conservative ageing population of working pensioners.

My host in Japan was a case example. His father, a man in his early eighties who has survived a multitude of health failures, had spent his life building up a portfolio of very successful businesses, ranging from an eyewear factory to a stable of regional magazines. The company still remained a family business, yet despite having a capable son and a daughter, both in their thirties, he remained reluctant to hand over the reins to the next generation. He continued to work eighty hours each week, which is regarded as completely normal in Japan, where it often seems that rather than being the means to some other end, work is the end in itself.

Whilst in the West publishing businesses have struggled to change their business models as print media has declined, in Japan the printed media remains buoyant, thanks to an older population who simply prefer to hold on to what they know and prefer, which is conventional printed media over the more versatile digital media. And so it is the older people of Japan who set the tone for the entire country, and younger people play something of a waiting game for the opportunity to shape and define their own world. But which are the more likely beta humans? Is it the old, insisting on a conservative and incremental adoption of human-improving innovations in order to avoid repeating past follies of too-rapid 'upgrading'? Or will it be the young, currently repressed in their ambition, who embrace the opportunity for Japan to again be the world's leading technological upgrader and improver?

Most jobs in Japan are currently styled as 'jobs for life' within large conglomerates. Many Japanese men refuse to retire, whilst their wives persist in fulfilling the societal expectation that they should be subservient homemakers and providers for all of their husbands needs in the kitchen and bedroom. Tradition and continuity are highly prized. But the trouble with this attitude is that it has also created a demographic time bomb. In 2017 the number of Japanese births dropped to 946,060, the lowest level since records began in 1899. That same year the number of deaths hit a post-war peak of 1.3 million. Japan's population fell by 394,373 people. In the 1970's Japanese women on average had 2.1 children each. In 2017 that number was only 1.4 – far below the rate at which Japan would maintain its population size. People over the age of 65 make up more than 25% of the population and adult diapers outsell baby diapers in supermarkets.

A positive take on this trend is that because young Japanese see their elders living until 90, they are putting off having children themselves until they reach their thirties when they have 'experimented' and 'found' themselves. 35 becomes the new 25. Except a 2016 government survey claimed that almost half of Japan's millennial singles aged between 18 and 34 were virgins. This lack of interest is blamed on everything from a stagnant economy where men earn a third of what they did during the boom years, to a new wave of professional women who see their subservient mothers and decide that marriage might just not be worth it after all. A preference for fantasy over reality is also blamed.

This is a big problem for would-be beta humans. Japan's tranquil, uber-respectful and well-ordered society cannot perpetuate or indeed evolve into the leading 'upgrader' that it once was if it's young people are uninterested or simply too polite to get drunk and fuck each other. So Japan remains split as a country. One the one hand Japan has kept a firmer grip on the traditions and conventions of its society and the invisible bonds that hold its society together remain strong even to the detriment of economic development. But Japan's refusal to wholly submit to the vogue of technological progress also creates conditions in which it is impossible to manifest beta humans.

In 'Man And Superman', George Bernard Shaw's devil suggests that all progress as we know it is merely the illusion of a great pendulum swinging backwards and forwards across periods of time that are greater than many human lifetimes. And for a Japanese person who has lived through the boom and then the "lost decades" this must feel very true, and is perhaps the impetus for staying still as a society despite the opportunities offered by the dawn of a new era of beta humans. What might be perceived as a resistance against rapid technological progress and the 'upgrading' of operating systems could equally be regarded as a collective and unspoken decision by the Japanese not to lose or sacrifice their values at a time when the rest of the world have sold out many of their conventions in the name of that same 'progress'. Because the Japanese have learned from the lost decades that followed their boom that this 'progress' can in fact be all-too-short-lived and entirely illusory.

The lesson here for beta humans is one of timing. The dawn of the beta humans relies on the epoch of the chain reaction of rapid technological progression being upon us now. Any attempt to usher or 'force in' the age of beta humans prematurely would lead to inevitable disappointments that would disenfranchise humans back into the status quo and comfort of standby mode. For the very first beta humans, timing is everything.

Thirty six hours into my unplanned self-experiment in sleep deprivation I found myself with my host in one of Tokyo's finest sushi bars. I did not yet know it, but it was to be the start of a week-iong assault of effusive hospitality that would teach me the very meaning of being crushed by kindness. The manners of my host were indisputably beyond reproach, and his English was native thanks to an early education in Great Britain and attending college in the USA. Education is highly prized in Japan. One late evening, my host and I returned to our hotel after a few bottles of wine, deep in inebriated conversation about the fact that he was a concert-level Cello player. When we arrived in the hotel I suggested that he should play some Cello for me some time, at which point he sat down at the grand piano in the hotel lobby and, entirely from memory, played the most beautiful and sophisticated piece of piano music that I have ever heard. It turned out that he was also a concert-level classical pianist. Neither of these musical skills were a prominent part of his character or ambition – they were simply a by-product of a very excellent and well-rounded education.

There is a common argument that the education system is the root of the failures of many Western nations to embrace the promises of technology in favour of iteratively patching operating systems for the next generation to deal with. The typical criticism of the modern Western education system is that schools are teaching young people what to think, instead of how to think. And as a result, many young people do not know how to spot objective truth amongst facts that might be presented to them as part of an often-hidden alternative agenda. Society thus starts to become a lame sponge that is woefully at the mercy of 'higher' authorities and their tendency to engage in cynical mass manipulation.

When I finished High School in 2001 I was happy to never have to look back at my fourteen years in a comprehensive - essentially socialist - education system in the UK which epitomized reversion-to-the mean.

Ambition was not so much not distilled in students as much as a lack of ambition, but thankfully there were many individual teachers who were happy to subvert this institutional impetus. For me it was the illuminating teaching of my history teacher Mr Finlay who opened up my eyes to the fact that history has already proven that literally anything can happen. Mr Finlay was a Scot who had lived in the midlands of England for such a long time that any accent was undetectable. He was an immensely well-educated man who had studied at St Andrews. The reasons that such a learned man had entered the vocation of teaching was never clear. He was probably the last of a generation who truly believed in teaching as a noble occupation.

From the ages of sixteen to eighteen I would spend three hours weekly amongst other budding historians in Mr Finlay's History class, and we all kept a great secret that I don't believe that the school ever discovered. That Mr Finlay had gone rogue. Rather than teach the insipid and limited history curriculum that was prescribed by the State, Mr Finlay had instead discretely turned his A-Level classes into University-style lectures in the classical traditionally-taught style that still exists at the Universities of Oxford, Cambridge, Durham and St Andrews. His few A-Level students would sit in a line on one side of the tables, whilst Mr Finlay sat back in a big chair on the other side and gave exquisite lectures that went far and beyond the scope of what was needed to pass exams. Mr Finlay was secretly giving his students something that the State education system was deliberately set up to deny them: a high quality classical education.

It is a sadness that I do not believe that there are many teachers today emulating Mr Finlay. That is not to say that there are not teachers out there with the same levels of verve. But teachers are now more highly-observed and closely-monitored in an education system which in Britain insists on pretending that all students should get exactly the same level of education, which leaves gifted students languishing in an insipid system. This is reflected in the relative proportions of privately-educated students at Britain's best Universities. Just

7% of under 16's and 18% of 16-18 year-olds in Britain go to fee-paying private (not provided by Government) schools. Yet 42% of the students at Oxford and 37% of students at Cambridge are drawn from private schools. Unless society has decided that the wealthy and monied are inherently more gifted and intelligent then their peers from poorer backgrounds, this is a scandal that eclipses all other social injustices in modern Britain.

In fact it is a compounding injustice, since the companies offering the most lucrative and stable career paths tend to recruit exclusively from these top Universities; truly ensuring that those wealthy enough to buy into the higher echelons of education continue to be treated as more inherently gifted than their poorer counterparts throughout their career and indeed throughout their life.

The operating system of education throughout the West is therefore one to which beta humans must bring a new age of enlightenment and upgrade. Even a technologically-upgraded society cannot grow great when it accepts such inequality in access to opportunity and social mobility.

As Mr Finlay taught his students, major changes in human history require conditions plus reasons and then a cause to 'spark' the change. The epoch of rapid technological development offers conditions. The social injustices of the most Western education systems and the disenfranchisement of Millennials (and younger generations) could provide the reasons. And beta humans could be the cause that unleashes technology to upgrade education systems so that every human being has the access to tailored and good-quality educational opportunities that unlock their full potential as human beings. This will be the litmus test as to whether a new age of human enlightenment has commenced and whether beta humans have successfully come into being.

I contemplated this thought in an expensive Tokyo sushi bar as I sat opposite the Itamae sushi chef. It can take up to twenty years for an Itamae to fully-master the art of sushi making, and it is Japanese legend that a truly-great master Itamae will be able to create nigirizushi in which all of the rice grains face in the same direction. It is hard to think of many other professions that require such an elongated and diligent period of training to achieve perfection. Some would say that to spend twenty years engaged in perfecting a skill that has no real impact on the world is a waste. But I think it's brilliant.

In the 1980's the British would joke about the Japanese and their intricately prepared dishes of raw fish. But by the 2000's Sushi was endemic in Britain. One of the most highly-rated restaurants in the world is a London sushi restaurant called Araki that seats just nine people. But the majority of sushi in Britain is now 'fast food' sushi that is pre-prepared and pre packed. It is sushi-in-name-only because it lacks high-quality fine ingredients and has not been prepared with the requisite skill.

I mention this because once that as a Westerner you travel into the realms of 'proper' sushi, prepared at great expense by one of Tokyo's finest Itamae, you realise that sushi is not as familiar to your palette as you expected. And so I found myself being diligently watched by my very excited host as I placed something that tasted like a sponge soaked in putrid vinegar into my mouth and, trying to hide my reticence, started chewing on it. I couldn't get any purchase between my teeth to break down whatever it was enough to end the ordeal by swallowing, and with each new attempt at chewing, more of the putrid vinegar squeezed into my mouth. After a while my eyes started watering and my gag reflex was quivering. But I revolved not to be disrespectful to the Itamae and to my host. To spit out the offending dish was not an option – it would have been a conspicuous indignity in the presence of the gentler sensibilities of the younger sister of my host.

The presence of my hosts younger sister was itself a curiosity. She was tall and beautiful and had also been educated in England before defying her family and spending her youngest years pursuing a career as an actress culminating in some stage performances of

Shakespeare in England. After a while her parents had decided that they would no longer support such free-spirited indulgence, and she had been summoned back home to be rewarded with a purse full of gold credit cards. She was now a canary trapped in a gilded cage, coerced into a conformity that was in defiance of her natural artistic character and temperament.

More curious was the reason that her brother had brought her along to co-host me for a few days. Ostensibly it was because she spoke English and had lived in Britain during her schooling, and so would be someone with whom I had enough in common to have a pleasant conversation with. But I had a clear sense that the darker underlying motivation of my 'agent provocateur' host was to tempt me into accepting a forthcoming offer to work for his family company in Tokyo by presenting his own sister as an indulgence that would be readily available to me if I accepted. At first I thought that perhaps my ego was getting the better of me in this reading of the situation, but as the week progressed I was left in no uncertainty that my hosts beautiful and very charming younger sister was a part of the 'package' being offered despite me having a fiancé (who is now my wife). When I have told male friends this story they have always nodded in approval. Female friends always respond with the same opinion of my male host: "what a total psycho!!"

But dodging the temptations on offer was the least of my problems as I continued to eat some of the world's best sushi. What I had expected to be an amazing experience had turned into a game of Russian roulette as each new dish arrived. Some dishes looked strange but tasted exceptional. Others looked normal but turned out to have weird flavours or textures that I had never previously experienced. The sense of trepidation as each piece entered my mouth was palpable.

Food can be an endless source of curiosity when you start your life growing up in a poor working class household but later find yourself in more affluent circumstances. It is also a source of amusement to consider those things that were barely-affordable luxuries when I was a child that are now cheap and ubiquitous. Take for example Vienetta, which launched in 1982 and is comprised of layers of vanilla ice cream sprayed upon layers of compound chocolate. Despite being made from poor quality ice cream and low-grade chocolate, amongst the families where I grew up a Vienetta was the height of expensive sophistication that was only to be served on very special occasions. Yet now you can buy a supermarket Vienetta for just £1, and it is standard fare in KFC and Pizza Hut. And there are other products with which I have the same relationship. A box of After Eight after-dinner mints were once a treat to be gifted at Christmas and then saved and slowly eaten at a rate of one after-dinner chocolate per day after a meal. Yet today a box can be bought for just £2. Orange Juice was once something that we bought in bulk in huge carboard cartons that would last for months and would even occasionally serve as a 'sophisticated' starter before a meal. Today it's a breakfast staple that must be freshly squeezed. Wine was bought in cardboard boxes for special occasions. Now a quality wine with good provenance is a daily staple for most households in the West.

Is it just me who finds amusement in this? Or has globalisation expanded the horizons of all people and made all of their worlds bigger too? What is certain is that when I managed to finish eating the finest Sushi that Tokyo had to offer, I felt like I had hit the plateaux of expanding the horizons of my own culinary world. All I could think about is how I'd love a box of After Eights right about now to rid me of the after taste.

My forty eight hours of sleep deprivation neared an end after my host gave me an extensive tour of Tokyo. At one point he excitedly took me to a well-regarded exhibition of Japanese pottery. I had to question whether this was a clever ruse by my host to punish the fact that my tiredness was fraying my resolve to be a courteous and enthusiastic recipient of his hospitality. Looking at vases whilst tired might just be the most perfect method for inducing sleep. Yet I had to steady myself and remain alert to prevent myself from falling asleep whilst still standing up. Eventually I took a taxi to my hotel, and was relieved to see a Starbucks nearby, where I could order some carbohydrate-rich food and sugar-laded snacks. It's easy to be snooty about Starbucks and to berate the quality of their coffee. But quite often when travelling, discovering a Starbucks is like finding an oasis whilst lost in the desert. It gives a moment of escape back into what you know. It might not offer the best coffee or sandwiches that money can buy, but it is reliably and comfortingly consistent.

My Tokyo hotel room was straight out of the 1980's, complete with floral curtains, carpets and duvet. I had wanted a double bed but the hotel only offered twin beds for reasons that remain a mystery. A clock and some buttons taken straight from the design of a Game Boy were built into the headboards of the bed, and I once again lamented how many years ago this would have been the pinnacle of brand new technology – screens and buttons in a bed – but that they now looked quite ridiculously old fashioned and obsolete. But at least my bathroom had a proper Japanese toilet.

Japanese toilets are a thing of a legend around the world and I am happy that the reputation holds true and is well deserved. Toilets that play music to you, heat the seat when you sit down, flash different colours, suck away bad smells and use an array of robotic arms and warm water jets to fulfil every need that one might have within the confines of a water closet, are commonplace. I am fairly sure that their functionality extends far beyond what I can describe, but I can't understand all of the Japanese buttons. It is becoming more common for higher-end hotels around the world to install and make a virtue of their Japanese-style toilets, and in fact my first encounter with one was at a hotel in Moscow. What is more of a mystery is why they have not caught on even more widely around the world by now?

The flushing toilet was invented by John Harington in 1596 and the first practical water closet was patented in England in 1778. But it is a man from South Yorkshire called Thomas Crapper who was responsible for popularising the toilet. Crapper & Co owned the world's first bath, toilet and sink showroom, which remained on King's Road in London until 1966. Crapper heavily promoted sanitary plumbing and pioneered the concept of the bathroom fittings showroom, which was rewarded in 1880 when Prince Edward, who would later become king, purchased Sandringham House in Norfolk and asked Thomas Crapper to supply thirty lavatories, which earned Crapper a Royal Warrant. This gave Crapper welcome notoriety, and by the time he died in 1910 he held nine patients for new and improved designs for toilets, which were a 'must have' for every family who valued social status. Manhole covers that give maintenance access to bathroom plumbing and bear the name of 'Crapper & Co' can still be seen in Westminster Abbey, where they are something of a fringe tourist attraction.

The basic toilet has barely changed since Thomas Crapper, except in Japan where the ultra-modern toilet first started to appear and then become ubiquitous in the 1980's. At first Japanese toilets were something of a joke to the Western world. But in a world where visiting a public lavatory can fill one with dread – especially in the United States where public lavatories are bizarrely constructed with extremely large gaps in the stalls to prevent illicit activity at the expense of everyone else's dignity – it now seems the Japanese have been having the last laugh from the very start.

The same applies with the famous Japanese bullet trains, where once again Japan was embracing beta-human-style upgrading many decades before any other nation. I found myself waiting to board my bullet train at a pleasant Tokyo railway station a few days after my arrival. A rail network is like the veins and arteries of a nation, moving people and talent and ideas around a country to facilitate and stimulate economic activity. Railways are not just the quickest way to travel distances of a few hundred miles, but also the most efficient, as they allow passengers to continue to go about their work as they glide across a country. In 1964 the first "high speed" railway line cut journeys between Tokyo and Osaka from six hours to just four. When the first Bullet Trains started to appear in the 1980's, the world joked about why trains needed to travel at 200mph. Today they are the undisputed envy of the world that most nations are still unable to emulate.

The country's Tokaido line, which runs from Tokyo to the city of Kobe, is the world's busiest railway line, carrying 150 million passengers each year. The average delay over the course of one year is less than one minute. When trains are delayed for five minutes, the conductor of a train must make a 'special announcement' and issue a "delay certificate" to all passengers on board. If a train is delayed for an hour, it makes national news. In 2017 the management of a rail company held a televised press conference to apologise after a train left a platform a full twenty seconds early.

The Tokyo railway station was busy but organised. I was issued with my ticket, which also told me where to stand on the platform so that I would board the correct carriage. When I found the right spot on the platform, there were different coloured lines to queue along depending on where my seat was positioned in the carriage, so that those who had to make their way to the centre of the carriage would board first to ensure maximum efficiency. Once aboard the train I was met by a man in an immaculate uniform that looked as sharp as he would have been at 9am on a Monday morning. He checked my ticket and showed me to my seat. The trains are extremely wide and so are the seats, which are big and comfy even in economy. Each seat can be rotated 180 degrees from its position, so that a group travelling together can opt to turn and face each other, or those wanting privacy can face forward in the more conventional way. And because the Japanese are staunchly respectful of one another, any conversations are conducted at only one decibel above a whisper. For someone to play music or videos on their phone, or to use headphones at a level that can be heard by others, is quite literally unheard of. It was blissful.

Bullet trains also offer some evidence that an aptitude for becoming the world's first beta humans has not diminished entirely from the Japanese during the lost decades. Construction is under way of the Chuo

Shinkansen, a maglev line between Tokyo and Nagoya that will reduce the 100-minute journey time to just 40 minutes. To get around the problem of Japan being a crowded island, 90% of the 178 mile maglev line will be built underground. The population may be shrinking, the economy may have lost two decades, young people might not be starting families, but Japan has not desisted from upgrading toward its own version of perfection when it comes to building railway infrastructure for the benefit of future generations.

There is also something unique in the make-up of Japanese society which means that the country has successfully embraced technology without sacrificing its humanity. This was evident when I arrived in the little-known Fukui Prefecture, an area that should be world-famous for its dinosaur fossils, its beauty, and as the ancient spiritual home of sushi and sake, but which barely registers on the tourist radar outside of Japan.

By now I was starting to get a full taste of polite and relentless Japanese hospitality. It started at breakfast each morning, where my host would insist on joining me at my hotel, where breakfast consisted of some cold cuts of smoked fish and little else more. Then as we were driven in a mini-van on the journeys of three-to-four hours a time around the Fukui Prefecture, my host would not leave me alone at peace for a single moment, fearful that to do so would mark him as an impolite and inhospitable host. The conversation was informed, entertaining and intelligent, but it was also relentless, punctuated only by lunch, which my host insisted must be a big restaurant affair with the finest Japanese food.

A few days into the trip the minivan pulled into a petrol station, and feeling starved of sugar and carbohydrates by my diet of healthy Japanese food, I stocked up on chocolate and candy and other sugar-rich treats. My host picked up on this and, slightly bemused, suggested "maybe we will have Western food for dinner tonight?". I am sure that the Japanese must find the Western predilection for chocolate and candy an absurdity. Most chocolate holds little or no nutritional value and serves only to store up longer-term health problems. Japan has the lowest rate of obesity of any OECD country with an obesity rate of 3.2% compared to Britain's 28% and the USA's 40%. The Japanese are simply too disciplined to sacrifice their long term health for a very short moment of sugar-based pleasure.

We arrived in a town that was famous for its thermal spas, and after staggering our way back from an alcohol fuelled dinner, my host suggested that we try the thermal spa in the hotel. We headed for what essentially looked like an indoor swimming pool, stripped down naked – you have to be naked because the colouring in swim shorts interfere with the purity of the water - and sat in the water without a single charge of homoeroticism and drank more wine whilst the water extracted the impurities from our bodies. Or was it adding minerals? Either way it must have been doing at least a little to offset some of the food and wine?

There is a stereotype that Japanese people cannot hold their alcohol, but the next morning at 8am my host was energetic and spritely and enthusiastic about keeping me entertained for another day, whilst I was fairly sure that I was going to die from my hangover. It turns out that drinking a lot, then sacrificing your hydration in a thermal bath, and then using nothing but litres of wine to rehydrate, is a very bad idea. I had hoped to get some sleep on the journey to Tojinbo, but my host once again insisted on keeping me engaged in conversation.

Tojinbo is a one kilometre long stretch of basalt cliffs along the Sea of Japan coast just north of Fukui City. The rocky coastline has been carved out by the waves, creating coarse pillar-shaped rocks that look like bundles of hexagonal and pentagonal rods in a geological formation that is unique in Japan. We arrived on a pleasantly warm day and there were hundreds of people sitting atop a nearby hill, presumably taking in the view. I walked to the hill expecting to be struck by the view of the cliffs below, but upon arriving I noticed that nothing of interest could be seen from this elevated position. The hundred-or-more people were not in fact taking in the view, but were glued to the screens of their smartphones. "Pokemon Go!" commented my host.

Pokeman Go it is an augmented reality smartphone game that uses GPS for players to locate and 'capture' virtual creatures called 'Pokemon'. When viewing somewhere through the camera of a mobile device, the game makes it appear as if the Pokemon is physically in the players real-world location. The objective is to capture, train and battle them with other players.

My first reaction on seeing the transfixed ignorance of more than a hundred people on their phones was overwhelmingly negative, but then I considered that, on the other hand, if it took chasing down fictional creatures within an augmented-reality game to persuade people to take more exercise and to visit more places of beauty and interest in the first place, then that can be no bad thing. Now we just need to get them to look up from the screen of their smartphones when they arrive. And it turned out that the crowds weren't really missing out on much. Tojinbo might be a natural curiosity within Japan, but it pales into insignificance once compared to Giants Causeway in Northern Ireland. In 1779 British literary giant Dr Samuel Johnson quipped that the Giants Causeway was "worth seeing, but not worth travelling to see". This assertion is undoubtedly wrong for the Northern Ireland landmark, but it unfortunately holds as accurate in regard to Tojinbo.

There is a beautiful continuity to people visiting natural landmarks like Tojinbo. These ritual visits connect humans to each other across the centuries in a way that technology cannot. The oldest church in England for example, has stood firm on its site in Canterbury since the year 597, and there are several other British churches that have stood since before the year 800.

Most Japanese temples are either monuments to a way of living or places of respectful spiritual contemplation and teaching. Rarely do they require unquestioning observance. The Heisenji Temple Hakusan Shrine for example sits on a mountain on a site dating to 717. It was once a temple to Hakusan worship, but was destroyed in a 1774 Buddhist uprising and later became a Hakusan Shrine. It is remarkable today because the site, on which just one building representing less than ten per cent of the original footprint that remains, is covered in a bright green moss that the monks have nurtured from the forest floor over many centuries. It is a place where one can feel spiritual without having a relationship with any particular God.

A more traditionally-Japanese temple is the Myotsuji Temple, which is surrounded on a hillside by thick Japanese cedar trees, quietly catching the sunlight that shines between them. It consists of a main temple building and a delectable three-storied pagoda, both of which are designated as national treasures. The pagoda once housed ancient scrolls depicting the early formation of what is now Japan by ancient emperors. The scrolls were attended to by monks for many centuries, but more recently have been moved into deep storage at the Fukui museum, who my host had persuaded to give us a private viewing – a very rare privilege. So I found myself stood deep within the restricted areas of the museum in a room that was separated from all natural light and kept cooled at a low temperature to protect the ancient scrolls. I donned a pair of plastic white gloves as the curators of the museum unravelled scrolls that were many hundreds of years old and featured exquisite drawing and painting depicting life in the earliest days of Japan. Art is the ultimate form of human expression. And to look at those scrolls, which were so rarely seen by human eyes, was to peer into the minds and the souls of the ancestors of Japan. It was exquisite. It also gave me an opportunity to try to perfect my bowing technique.

Showing respect sits at the top of Japanese social priorities and manifests itself in an endless procession of bowing, in particular in the presence of older people, who must be respected for their age and wisdom and the assumed great accomplishments that can be attained when living a long life. When I had first arrived in Japan, my host had suggested that it was not necessary or expected that I would bow, but as the trip had progressed I had felt increasingly awkward standing doing nothing whilst my host repeatedly bowed throughout conversations with the various Japanese people who had assisted us gain access to temples and shrines and now to the ancient scrolls in the museum. Not bowing was starting to feel a little like going through life without saying thank you for acts of kindness, and it didn't sit well not to make an effort.

The problem with bowing is that it flies in the face of Western customs. If you shake someone's hand or want to show them gratitude, then the most important part of that interaction is the eye contact. Eye contact conveys transparent sincerity and mutual respect for one another as fellow human beings. And so to bow to someone is to break that eye contact, and to do so repeatedly is to undertake an act without being able to see any reaction. What's more, the greater your gratitude and respect, the longer and deeper that your bow must be, which extends the period of possible embarrassment if, for some reason, you are getting your bow wrong, not to mention the social awkwardness that comes from the uncertainty of now knowing if you have given a sufficient bow to reflect the commensurate level of respect and gratitude that you should be conferring upon the recipient. Bowing is thus fraught with myriad opportunities for unintended consequences.

When I had first encountered my host endlessly bowing throughout conversations, I had found it a little unusual that polite society required him to revert to these submissive acts of contrition. I perceived that polite Western society was about recognising each other on an equal footing, whilst Japanese society seemed to be about submission and deference. But I soon came to realise that what might at first seem like an act of weakness is in fact one of strength. To bow in respect or gratitude is not to submit oneself into a permanent subordinate position, but a powerful act of humility which applies only to that specific moment in time. It takes a lot of discipline and control of ones ego to make a momentary display of deference, but that also means that it has an authenticity and sincerity that is completely unmistakable. And so after spending an hour or more gently pawing over the ancient scrolls, I unleashed a campaign of gracious bowing onto the museum curators, who seemed bemused but also appreciative of my attempts to make an effort. Yes it was strange relative to what I was used to, but that was not grounds for condemnation, because clearly the convention is a successful one in a Japan, where people still show a lot of respect for each other. And I also felt a little ashamed that I had been so slow on the uptake by not embracing the custom much earlier.

My penultimate day in Fukui Prefecture ended at the Eiheiji Temple, a Soto Zen training monastery established in 1244 by Gogen Zenji, the founder of Soto Zen Buddhism in Japan. We were met by a handsome-looking six-foot-tall monk dressed entirely in black robes with a bald head and a very big smile of shiny white teeth. He was extremely well built and his black robes were tied with a rope around his middle that gave him even more presence. I couldn't help thinking that he looked more like some kind of secret ninja who could easily conceal several swords within his robes, but his endless smiles and general sense of happiness and positivity with his world belied any sense that he was not what he appeared, which was a very happy and contented individual.

Zen Buddhism offers a counterbalance to the mission of beta humans. By relying heaving on technology Beta humans aim to achieve collective human betterment by upgrading everything about the world in which all humans must exist – the world's operating systems – and to reveal greater human meaning and purpose. By contrast, Zen Buddhism seeks to reprogram the internal software of each individual human so that she or he can exist in better harmony with an operating system (the Zen belief system) that does not expect or require the world to provide betterment, but harmony and peace. This is the inherent dichotomy of Japan – whether human betterment and enlightenment are best-found in the embrace of technology, or in its total divestiture.

We walked past a huge outdoor gong with the power to wake up everything and anything from miles around, and I had to work hard to resist the temptation to pull back and release the horizontally-suspended tree trunk that could be used to sound it. The monk welcomed us into what I had come to recognise as a typically traditional room: it was modest with woven mats on the floor. We kneeled side-by-side and the monk guided my host and I through a Chaji tea ceremony, which was then followed by a ceremonial Shojin Ryori feast, which is comprised of food that is consumed by Zen monks because it is low in calories and healthy.

The Shojin Ryori feast is served in a series of red trays on the ground. Each tray has its own square compartments containing a modest amount of something, and a small bowl for soup and another for rice are included at the side. It is said that apart from taste and flavour, you can feel the four seasons manifested in every dish with your five senses, and since the entirety of the feast is vegetarian, I felt on safer ground than I had been at the Sushi bar in Tokyo.

The ceremonial aspect involved lifting the bowls up with extended arms and holding them out in appreciation, before breathing them in and placing them courteously down again. It was a long winded way to eat but there was something in it. As humans we rely on the earth and the seasons for all of our food and sustenance, yet thanks to huge global supply chains and supermarkets, we take it all for granted. Rarely do we pause and take time to be thankful for the abundance of food available in modern society or to feel a sense of appreciation for it, and we really should, because it requires a humility that is often lacking in humans.

As we prepared to leave I respectfully asked the Monk if we could take a photo together, and he smiled broadly as I snapped a selfie with my smartphone. Seconds later he pulled out his own smartphone – the latest iPhone model with a huge touch screen – from his robes, and he took some photos too. Clearly even someone dedicated to the pursuit of spiritual oneness still needed Facebook; and technology still proved a life enhancing necessity for even the most avid student of Zen.

About 22% of Japanese work more then 49 hours a week, compared to 16% of Americans and 11% of French and Germans. Less than half of the vacation days allotted to Japanese workers are ever taken, because employees fear resentment from co-workers if they take days off, which is a valid concern in a conformist culture that values harmony. In 2016 new laws were introduced to force the Japanese to take more holidays after a spate of cases of professionals who quite literally worked themselves to death.

This relentless work ethic is a problem for would-be beta humans in Japan. To create and innovate, humans must be able to take their experiences and use them to synthesise new things. But if most humans are too busy working to have new experiences, then a society has no basis for the creative ingenuity that is required to upgrade a country's many operating systems. The problem runs deep in Japan, which is regularly ranked as one of the least entrepreneurial countries in the world. The Japanese have given bureaucratic jobs the highest prestige and adopt a "funnel to the top" policy that is based not on ingenuity but on broadest experience and longest service. This leads talented individuals to put in many hours of face time at their offices chasing membership of this elite bureaucracy, rather than engaging in entrepreneurial invention and ingenuity. This is despite huge demand for investment opportunities from Japanese households who have the highest rate of savings in the world but with low and even negative interest rates on those savings.

This again highlights the dichotomy at the core of the Japanese psyche. The Japanese propensity for deliberate ritual and for acknowledging the 'life energy' in every action and sensation makes one feel more alive, and is perhaps why the Japanese literally have more 'life force' than most nations. The Japanese live to an average age of 84 compared to 81 in Britain and 79 in the USA. But the Japanese also embrace a punishing working life that seems in conflict with Zen.

This matters for beta humans. For over two millennia, and throughout the last century, religion has played a key role in binding all humans into the collective endeavour of elevating themselves out of the darkness and into our enlightened age of technology. Yet by definition the endeavour of beta humans is a humanist one. There is no doubt that Japan's social structures and the underlying influence of Zen have protected a society which remains unequivocally grounded in respect, good manners and treating each other well in expectation of receiving the same in return. And Japan also has some of the hallmarks for beta humans in its attitude to building technologically advanced railways.

But the overwhelming sense that you get from Japan is of a wonderfully talented and well-educated country that can't quite get its act together, because it does not know whether to embrace the forward-looking promises of technology or to embrace the backward-looking promises of Zen. Japan doesn't yet have an operating system that works and it is not yet willing to experiment with alternative recipes, especially since the last 'experiment' led to the 1989 crash that precipitated the loss of two decades. Japan is still trying to define itself in an ever changing modern world, unsure of the place of its ancient civilisation in the new world order. This dichotomy must be resolved for its beta humans to rise.

SINGAPORE

The British Military Hospital in Singapore is not on most tourist itineraries. In February 1942 Japanese Imperial Forces occupied Singapore after defeating the combined British, Indian, Australian and Malayan garrison in the Battle of Singapore. The garrison defending the island surrendered after just one week of fighting in what Winston Churchill called "the worst disaster and largest capitulation in British history". As the British First Malaya Infantry Brigade retreated, they sought cover from within the perceived safety of the British Military Hospital. Among the patients in the hospital were the surviving crew members of the Force Z British naval squadron, an ill-fated convoy of ships that had sought to deter the Japanese military advance, but were ill-prepared for engagement by the Japanese from the air. With no Allied air support, the HMS Prince of Wales and HMS Repulse had been easily sunk by Japanese torpedo bombers on the tenth day of December in 1941, just three days after the Japanese attack on Pearl Harbour. Of the 1,612 officers and men aboard the Prince of Wales, 327 died. The toll on Repulse was higher at 513 from a complement of 1,309. In total 840 souls were blown apart by torpedoes and bombs or scalded to death by escaping steam or ripped to shreds on the exposed undersides of the stricken titans. Many drowned while awaiting rescue or became trapped in the watertight compartments that became their tombs. Admiral Sir Tom Phillips, commander of Force Z, chose to remain to the end on the bridge of the Prince of Wales, his flagship.

The survivors of the sinking were taken to the British Military Hospital in Singapore, but as they lay in their beds alongside other military casualties, the Japanese advanced on the hospital. A lieutenant from the British Infantry Brigade was sent with a Red Cross brassard and a white flag of surrender to meet with the Japanese troops and announce the surrender of the civilians. But he was killed immediately. The Japanese troops then rushed the hospital and bayoneted 250 patients and staff members to death. A further 400 patients and staff were locked up in a small room where many died from

269

suffocation. Those who survived the initial ordeal were removed from the room in small groups and summarily shot, their bodies buried in mass graves. Only a handful of people managed to survive the massacre.

On 6 August 1945 the United States detonated their atomic bomb over the Japanese city of Hiroshima followed on 9 August by another atomic bomb that was dropped on Nakasaki. And on 15 August, the Japanese surrendered. After a period of anomie British troops were met with cheering and fanfare when they arrived in Singapore once again, and it was another eighteen years before Britain ceded its sovereignty over Singapore to Malaysia and another two years before Singapore become independent on 9 August 1965.

Today the British Military Hospital in Singapore is known as 'Alexandra Hospital' and it is part of the National University of Singapore's medical school. As I approached it had an eerie quietness about it. There didn't seem to be anybody around and it didn't have the kind of bustle that you would associate with a hospital.

It held a tranquil position amidst lush green gardens, the hospital gates were open, and there appeared to be no security as I casually ventured in to take a look around.

One of the great things about having a British accent is that it affords you a great spectrum of opportunities to escape punishment for polite disobedience. Most authorities will give an (entirely undeserved) deference to intelligent lexicon and clear British diction. One summer I visited the monumental Blenheim Palace in Oxfordshire, which is an exquisite and ornate palace inspired by Versailles that was built in the early eighteenth Century for the Duke of Marlborough to mark his victory over the French in the War of Spanish Succession. My wife and I arrived at Blenheim very early in the morning, and we were pleased to find almost no other people around. The massive front doors to the Palace were closed, so I turned the door handle and walked inside. We passed a few staff who were busy going about their business, but otherwise the Palace was deserted and we had it entirely to ourselves.

After an hour inside we exited into the main courtyard as a pleasant and official-looking elderly lady approach us with a big smile. "The Palace will be opening in five minutes" she said, "If you join the line now you'll avoid the crowds that come later on". We thanked the lady for her advice and went to find some tea, pleased to be in a country where the worst that can happen when you turn a handle and innocently walk through a door that you're not supposed to is that you might be politely asked to leave, but more likely is that if you are behaving respectfully, you will go entirely unnoticed.

I was hopeful to go equally unnoticed in the grounds of the former British Military Hospital in Singapore. My younger brother is a C17 Captain in the Royal Air Force, and when on layover in Singapore had also made this pilgrimage to the Alexandra Hospital for the very same reason that I was: because it is where our mother was born in 1950. My brother had found a plaque in the gardens marking the history of the former Military Hospital and had taken a photo of himself there that I was hoping to emulate, and after a bit of walking around and searching, I was able to find the plaque amidst some plants within a pretty memorial garden.

After taking a photo I preceded to the main entrance of the hospital, which aside from the addition of a modern-entrance canopy looked little different to how it was depicted in the old pictures that I had seen. As I stood in front of the building taking more pictures, two security guards came hurtling toward me, one of them shouting into his radio, whilst a third appeared behind me as if from nowhere and grabbed hold of the back of my t-shirt. They asked what I was doing taking pictures of the building, and were a little surprised when I explained that the hospital is where my mother was born, so I was taking a few pictures to send to her. The guards all looked at each other, unsure what to do. My useful British accent was clearly dissuading them from action, as one of them turned to me to tersely explain than "It is against the law to take pictures of public buildings!". Another of the guards was busily talking on his radio, informing somebody that they had

273

"control" of the situation and asking someone to "stand by" and to be ready to call the Police.

For the entire forty minutes or more that I had been unwittingly 'trespassing' within the hospital grounds, not a single vehicle had come or gone, but as luck would have it, as the guards argued about what to do, a blue Singapore taxi pulled under the canopy and some passengers got out and went inside. The taxi driver looked over to me, hopeful that I might be his next fare, so I opened the door to the taxi and jumped in. "Drive!" I politely requested, as the security guards looked on with surprise as the taxi sped away. They could have given chase, or closed the gates to the grounds before I could reach them, but I got the sense that the security guards were equally pleased that they no longer had to decide what to do.

This might seem like an overreaction to a tourist taking a few photos, but this unwaveringly rigid application of the rules is part of the recipe that has turned Singapore into the world's premiere technology nation, albeit a very small one. For decades the City-State of Singapore has been entirely preoccupied with the physical upgrade of every aspect of itself, and as a consequence, its economy and quality of life have leaped decades ahead of its competitors. Singapore has become famous for its impeccable cleanliness and for its crime rate, which is so low that the country recently had to put out a warning to remind people that "low crime does not mean no crime" - and to stay vigilant.

Not that the locals pay too much heed to this message. At the centre of Singapore's financial district, nestled between the glass and steel skyscrapers, is Lau Pa Sat, a historic covered market building with a Victorian cast-iron structure designed by James MacRitchie and crafted in Glasgow by Walter MacFarlane & Company; and which has many similarities to the famous Victorian-built Leadenhall and Borough markets in London. Lau Pa Sat houses a huge number of street-food stalls and is the central hub for working Singaporeans to get a quick lunch. The market is furnished with hundreds of tables and chairs, and the convention is that a group of colleagues will find a table with some space, and then place something on the table to "save" the seats whilst they each go to different food stalls to collect their lunches, which they then enjoy whilst seated together. Typically Singaporeans will place a packet of tissues on the table in front of each seat to 'reserve' it, but on more than one occasion I saw groups place and leave smartphones on the tables instead. The system was respected by all and worked very well. But more remarkable is that Singapore is considered so safe that locals can leave a collection of smart phones unattended in a busy public place and be confident that they will still be there when they return.

This sense of orderly respect combined with low crime is one reason why Singapore is known as "The Fine City". The other reason is because the city imposes many punishing fines for non-conformity. Chewing gum is banned in Singapore with a $1,000 fine for possession. Littering with items like drinks cans or cigarette butts or candy wrappers come with a $300 dollar fine and a 'Corrective Work Order' that requires the offender to clean up the specified area wearing a luminous green vest. Smoking is banned in all public spaces and elevators are equipped with urine detection devices that detect the scent and set off an alarm then lock the doors to trap the assailant still inside until the Police arrive. Vandalism including graffiti is a serious offense punishable by caning and jail time. The Police are authorised to run random drug tests on locals and visiting foreigners who face fines, jail and even deportation if they have drugs in their system. The treatment for drug smugglers is particularly inhospitable: they are executed. Not that young Singaporeans are likely to grow up into a life of crime, because parental discipline is also tough, with caning still widespread. Parents can buy a thin rattan cane with a plastic hook in most local supermarkets.

Whilst at first this might sound like a dystopian nightmare, if you are actually one of the 99.99% of people who respects your local community and is polite and courteous in your behaviours, then the outcome of the universal application of these rules is a beautiful city that appears to be channelling Ronald Reagan's "shining city". Singapore is clean, almost crime free and is extremely pleasant to experience. This matters for beta humans, because Singapore shows that by upgrading everything – from infrastructure to social systems – it is indeed possible to elevate all humans and to create betterment far beyond the limitations of the internal software of individual human beings. Singapore shows that the world of the beta humans is not an idealised fantasy, but is eminently possible.

The challenge for beta humans is to take the Singapore model and apply it in much larger countries and communities where current conventional wisdom demands that exceptions must be made to accommodate different 'tribes' of humans. But Singapore has already shown that this deference to the 'exceptionalism' of tribalism does not always lead to overall human betterment. A 2017 nationwide study by the Singapore Institute of Policy Studies found that class boundaries tend to be far more salient than tribal boundaries such as gender, race or religion. So Singapore makes major investments in ensuring that every single child has access to a very high quality education. One study showed that the proportion of children in Singapore's poorest 20% who later in life find themselves in the richest 20% is higher than in the United States or Denmark, and that by 2016 income inequality in Singapore had already fallen to its lowest in a decade. Put more simply, by upgrading its entire operating system without pandering to the current vogue for segmenting populations into individual tribes based on identity, Singapore has accelerated social mobility and created unprecedented new levels of human betterment that have positively impacted its entire population.

Perhaps one of the greatest stories of social mobility in Singapore comes from its greatest unofficial cultural institution. In the late 1970's Madam Ong Kim Hoi started a small seafood stall in Singapore. It was very common in those days for hawker stalls to sell fresh seafood and crab dishes. Madam Hoi had a penchant for cooking and created a White Pepper Crab dish using a recipe that still remains a closely-guarded family secret even today. This extra-special dish won wide acclaim and differentiated the hawker stall from the competition. And since the stall had no name and no sign board to identify it, it became known locally as 'the stall with no signboard', and then 'no signboard'.

The first 'no signboard' restaurant opened in 1990, and today it is a leading chain of seafood restaurants in Singapore. It is led by the grandchildren of Madam Hoi, who are known for their high-spending and their largesse when buying expensive supercars. Whilst this is not exactly a fairy tale ending, it is a good example of the kind of mobility that Singapore hopes to create: the poor in society rising to be amongst the richest within a single generation. And the White Pepper Crab at No Signboard, whilst a little on the expensive side, is spectacular. I visited with friends and we committed to a fixed menu "feast" that was astonishingly good. The crab is killed-to-order in the restaurant, and the accompanying sauces and other dishes are so creamy and indulgent that any initial embarrassment about having to wear a large plastic bib whilst eating soon fades into obscurity compared to the culinary pleasure. And to be fair, the bib is needed, because eating fresh seafood and shell fish is a very messy business.

I was joined in this feast at No Signboard by my wife and a few friends, and whilst breaking open crab claws and messily removing the tasty white meat from inside, our conversation turned to the axiom of rules that seemed to preserve the polite integrity of Singaporean society. Having enjoyed a couple of beers with our food, I posed the subject of what social rules we would all create and enforce in our own countries if we were in charge. To demonstrate I quickly reeled off my own list of rules, and it turned out that I have significantly more authoritarian tendencies than I had realised. Here are some of the people that I would like to see fined or jailed 'Singapore-style' for breaking my own regime of rules: People who stand on the left on the escalators on the London Underground. People who walk around with no spatial awareness because they are wearing headphones. People who spoil the tranquillity of public parks and beaches by playing music. People who drive fast in built up areas where children live. People who drive too slowly on the highway. People who 'vape' and leave lingering vapour clouds behind them that other people have to walk through. People who shout in public. People who think an opinion is as valid as a fact. Young men who put their hands down their trousers in public as if it's normal. People who never read a book. People who get too excited by memes.

After gorging at No Signboard I decided to complete another part of my Singapore mission: to drink a Singapore Sling in The Long Bar at Raffles Hotel. The Singapore Sling is a gin based cocktail that was invented by a Hainanese bartender at The Long Bar around 1915. Sipping the cocktail at The Long Bar surrounded by the sumptuous surroundings whilst throwing peanut shells onto the floor is long-established trope on the bucket list of every Singapore traveller. The bar oozes 1920's sophistication and style, which is accentuated by the mechanised ceiling and wall fans. I'd like to think of my grandparents sitting at the bar in a lounge suit and a cocktail dress, sipping Singapore

Slings before some military function. Except by the time that my grandparents lived in Singapore they had four young children and my grandfather was blocked from promotion in the British army because he had "gone native" by marrying an Indian woman, so whilst I like to nurture the fantasy, it is unlikely that my grandparents social standing would have availed them to having drinks within The Long Bar at Raffles. But it is very easy to imagine the bar when it was smoke filled, the crunch of empty peanut shells underfoot, the heat of the night only temperately cooled by the mechanised fans as the customers dreamed wistfully of the cooler nights of England's green and pleasant land.

There are two problems with trying to recreate that feeling today. The first is that Singapore's strict anti-smoking laws mean that the air inside The Long Bar is crisp and clean, so you can clearly see every detail from one side of the bar to the other. This means it's hard to truly recapture the traditional atmosphere, which would have been thick with twisting patterns of smoke rising from tobacco pipes and cigarettes to obscure the view.

Secondly, because it has become a popular 'bucket list' thing to do, The Long Bar is much like a tourist attraction in China: droves of people sit on the bar stools and at the tables sipping Singapore Slings and hoping to experience its colonial heyday, except by virtue of the bar being filled with fellow tourists this is simply not possible. So most visitors take a few photos with their Singapore Sling and then leave having posted them online and geo-tagged The Long Bar. Tick.

The Long Bar is one of just a few exceptions to Singapore's relentless zeal for upgrading. Building a clean and crime free society with healthy levels of one-generation social mobility seemingly requires this constant drive to improve and upgrade everything in order to elevate people's lives. And it seems to be working. And as of 2017, eighty of the world's top 100 technology firms had operations in Singapore thanks to it being a geopolitical safe haven with a vast array of international free trade agreements in place and a geographical position at the heart of Asia.

In an important contrast to the West Coast of the United States, Singapore's technology titans are actively invited to participate in building the country and maintaining the status of the City-State as the world's pre-eminent 'smart city'. Policymakers routinely invite technology firms with a footprint in Singapore to participate in problem-solving and capacity-building exercises. One example is a project called 'Virtual Singapore', which is building a one-to-one scale 3D digital model of the entirety of the city to include an accurate representation of everything on the island including vegetation, piping, cabling and even air ducts and trash chutes. This might sound absurd, but it means that Governments and private companies can model outcomes and focus on upgrading projects that will deliver the best return. When you know the dimensions of a rooftop for example, it's possible to calculate and model whether a block has the space to power itself entirely from solar power. This means that the Government in Singapore is less likely to embark on projects that turn out to be expensive white elephants.

Another project already under development is 'Vehicle To Everything' which is also known as 'V2X'. V2X allows cars, traffic lights, road signs and security cameras to seamlessly communicate with one another. Soon cameras at pedestrian crossings will be able to tell cars that pedestrians are ahead of them before the driver – or autonomous car – sees them. Traffic lights and road signs will be able to self-regulate the flow of traffic around the city and to clear the path for emergency vehicles. When it comes to a bold vision for a brave new future powered by the latest infrastructure and technologies to the benefit of all citizens, Singapore is simply way out in front. Britain might have been the father of the industrial revolution and the United States the powerhouse of Twentieth century capitalism, but at the dawn for the Fourth Industrial Revolution - which will bring together digital, biological and physical technologies in powerful combinations – it is Singapore that is ranked by the World Economic Forum as the best-prepared to recoup the benefits from this brave new world.

The Singaporean Government invests the equivalent of 1% of its annual GDP into technology projects. In 1991 that amounted to £1 billion. By 2017 it amounted to £10.4 billion. And that set off an exponential chain reaction by attracting the world's best technological researchers and innovators who were eager to see their ideas get funded and realised, thus further entrenching and expanding Singapore's advantage and turning the city-state into a self-fulfilling prophecy where rapid progress begat even more progress. Every new piece of new 'smart' technology is adopted with the purpose of improving the lives of everyone in Singaporean society. The city-state is therefore a real life manifestation of the hypothetical promise of the technology titans of the West Coast USA: it is applying technology to overcome the impediments to upgrading into a better society.

As if to point out the difference in attitude and outlook between an Asian Tiger like Singapore and the 'elder statesmen' Western nations like Britain and the USA, I had pulled some favours and managed to arrange an unofficial behind-the-scenes tour of the Rolls Royce jet engine factory in Singapore. The engineering titan employees 22,300 people in Britain, which makes its Singapore facilities (that first opened in 1950) seem relatively modest by comparison with just 2,300 employees. However the Singapore facility, which manufactures fan blades and assembles jet engines, is truly state-of-the-art. Rolls Royce has local partnerships with Singapore's top Universities and Government agencies, and in 2006 was given Singapore's 'Distinguished Partner in Progress Award' – the nation's highest corporate honour. Yes, Singapore hands out honorary accolades that recognise *companies* who make a tangible contribution to building and upgrading their country. The city-state is not just bringing technology companies in to participate in nation building – it also gives them official recognition for the contribution that they make to upgrading the world in which Singaporeans must exist.

The Rolls Royce jet engine is an enduring symbol of ingenuity and design, and touring the company's factory in Singapore was jaw-droppingly awesome. A single Rolls Royce Trent engine is made from 30,000 individual components. At take off a pair of Trent 1000s will deliver thrust of 150,000 lbf – which is equivalent to the power of 1,500 cars. The 112-inch fan blades spin at over 900mph, but the blades inside the engine itself can top 1,200 mph. To see several of these engines stripped of their coverings and to gaze upon their infinite complexity is to observe the pinnacle of the achievements of modern-day humans. Each engine is put together by hand by highly skilled engineers at a cost to the final customer of $10 million. In 2015 the Singapore facility assembled 80 engines and 3,100 fan blades. By 2017 the facility was producing 250 engines and 8,600 blades each year.

In the months before visiting Singapore I had also toured the Boeing factory just outside Seattle and the Airbus factory, which is located just south of Paris. They were both impressive, but their environments had felt more like engineering workshops than places of high-technology. Their employees looked casual and individualistic: they looked like men and women who knew what they were doing with a welder and some metal during the day and who would happily enjoy drinking a beer whilst listening to some music (Seattle) or having an evening with their mistress (Paris) after a hard day of heavily-unionised (Paris) work. By contrast the pristine white and surgically-clean Rolls Royce engine factory was like stepping into the future. The workers were younger and they all looked well-presented and wore branded overalls. And they seemed entirely engaged in what they were doing – like being an engineer was what they lived a breathed for every moment of their life. It was that which defined who they are, and they were eminently proud of it. The workers at Rolls Royce in Singapore were creating works of engineering art more efficiently than anywhere else in the world. And to the untrained eye they appeared to be literally generations ahead.

Singapore also benefits vastly from something that former British Prime Minister Margaret Thatcher advocated for in her final great literary work 'Statecraft': being a tariff free port. The publication of

Statecraft arose from Lady Thatcher's concern that in the age of spin doctors and sound bites, the ever-present danger was that political leaders would follow fashion and not their instincts and beliefs. Her advocacy of Britain becoming a tariff-free port had a firm logic which Singapore has long-since proven. As a free port and open economy, more then 99% of all imports into Singapore enter the country duty free. 100% of imports from the USA are tariff free. And 80% of the goods imported into Singapore will eventually be exported again to the rest of the world, because companies can easily use Singapore's free trade area to store, sort, assemble, modify and then re-export their products. The consequence of this is that with a domestic population of less than six million, Singapore has developed major industries that are internationally competitive. 59% of exports are of machinery and transport equipment. 16.5% is chemical products and 15% is manufactured goods and articles. The nation-state ranks third in the world behind only Liechtenstein and Hong Kong with exports per capita of $63,700. By contrast Great Britain ranks 34th with $7,376 and the United States languishes at 46th with $4,900.

By allowing products and materials to flow freely in and out of its ports without seeking to impose tariffs, Singapore has turned itself into the perfect location for the kind of manufacturing industries that are popular with Western voters. Singapore imports the world's raw materials, turns them into products, and then exports them back to the world. The population of the city-state is equivalent 0.08% of the population of Great Britain, but its exports are equivalent to 85%. 85%!

Back at Rolls Royce Singapore, as I waited for a taxi in the large reception of the facility, my host suggested that it was a tradition for guests to have their photo taken in front of a huge fan blade that stood alone like a piece of sculpture behind some velvet ropes in the reception area. Happy to oblige this tradition, I posed ready for a picture, but my host took one look through my camera lens and declared that the fan blade looked too dusty, and that this was not acceptable, not even for a photo that would only ever be seen by me. Much commotion then followed. The receptionists declared themselves unable to dust off the fan blade, so they contacted 'facilities'. 'Facilities' deemed that they weren't allowed to touch it for health and safety reasons, and that it was the responsibility of the third-party building management firm. The building management firm decreed that cleaning was the responsibility of the cleaning agency that they subcontracted out to, and that somewhere in the building was a man with a mop and bucket who worked for minimum wage at the bottom of this vast chain of managers. Unfortunately, nobody knew where he was, and nobody else wanted to risk their position or liability by undertaking to dust off the fan blades themselves. So I asked if they could find me a cloth, which they did, and I ducked under the protective ropes to give the fan blades a good dusting off as the crowd of people who were now involved in this activity looked on nervously. It is a curious phenomenon that middle management has an in-built propensity to perpetuate itself to the

293

point that there can be several layers of 'management' in place simply to govern the work of a solitary cleaner.

Every night in Singapore the tourist crowds flock to watch the camp-fest that is the daily Garden Rhapsody music and light show underneath the iconic 'Super Trees' in the Gardens By The Bay. The gardens represent another way in which Singapore is exhibiting the kind of behaviours that could signal the dawn of the beta humans. The trend for building public parks and green spaces first started in London in 1845 when Victoria Park was opened because 30,000 people, led by sanitary reformer William Farr, signed a petition calling for Queen Victoria to open a space for working class families to get fresh air. This was not an entirely selfless act by the middle class signatories: they were concerned that a lack of fresh air would worsen the incidence of cholera, typhus and tuberculosis in the poverty-stricken slums, and that this disease would start to spread out into their own middle class neighbourhoods. More public parks followed in Battersea and Finsbury, created to the similar design motif of sweeping lakes, bandstands and pavilions. The Victorian penchant for vigorous fresh air, constitutional walks and improving the lot of the working poor meant that around the same time Regents Park was also opened to the public for relaxation, leisure and entertainment; and soon all eight Royal Parks in London followed suit. The Victorians were also acutely aware of the power of trees to absorb pollution, and so they planted trees along residential and commercial streets with a great zeal that is matched in magnitude only by the zeal of their modern day local government contemporaries to have those same trees cut down. The Victorians were so successful in their endeavours that modern London is made of 40% public green space including more than 3,000 parks covering 35,000 acres. Some of those acres date back to the dissolution of the monasteries by Henry VIII, but their availability for the public to enjoy without cost, and their layout and facilities, are a Victorian contrivance.

Singapore's great public park at Gardens By The Bay spans 250 acres and is part of the Government's forward-looking strategy to transform Singapore from a "Garden City" to a "City in a Garden". Designed by British architecture firms Grant Associates and Dominic White, the park includes huge modernist conservatories, an indoor cloud forest, a flower dome and paths that snake and wind through pretty and well-maintained gardens. I particularly enjoyed the indoor cloud forest, a huge conservatory that claims to emulate the cool moist conditions of tropical mountain regions, but serves as a pleasant and cool relief for Britons like me who are not used to Singapore's humid conditions.

The undisputable centrepiece of the gardens is the iconic Supertree Grove. The Supertrees are tree-like concrete-and-steel structures that are up to 50 metres in height and which dominate the garden landscape. They were designed as "vertical gardens" that perform many functions including planting, shading and working as environmental engines for the gardens. Unsurprisingly given their 'smart city' location, the trees are much more that urban sculpture. Each is fitted with environmental technologies that mimic the ecological function of trees, including photovoltaic cells that harness solar energy, which is then used to power their lighting. There is a moment in human evolution when the ancestors of humans descended from the trees to walk upon the ground. And if Singapore continues its technology-driven upgrading, then the first beta humans might emerge from the crucible of Supertree Grove.

Prospective beta humans will notice obvious parallels between Singapore and Dubai. Both cities are placing their future development firmly in the hands of new and emerging technologies. Both still maintain prejudicial and discriminatory policies on important matters of civil rights that are entirely incongruous with their ambitions to be global leaders. Both are relatively small by global standards. And both favour a built environment that is manicured and pristine. Both are modelling themselves as great trading nations. Both are modelling themselves as gateways between East and West, although Singapore is doing it through free trade policies whereas Dubai relies on low tax rates. And yet they both also lack something esoteric and intangible.

Singapore feels sanitised and synthetic. It is almost too clean, too polished, too measured and too middle class. I had a strong feeling that all of the smart-city technologies that were making life better for everyone meant that Singapore was also at risk of losing that very important esoteric thing: its soul. Taken to its natural conclusion, Singapore could one day offer its citizens seemingly perfect lives. People might be able to service most of their needs online, but this would reduce the opportunities for serendipity that come from human interaction. They might be able to travel with incredible efficiency across the city-state using public transport systems that are clean and efficient to the nearest second, and spend money in malls that they've earned in a nation with some of the world's best rates of social mobility. But something would still be missing.

Venice by contrast, is the most alluring city in the world because of the beauty and decay that is visible everywhere. Venice is a great seducer with a hypnotic charm, risen like Venus from the waves and always threatening to sink again. Far from embracing modernity, Venice stands still: a Venetian of the 16th Century would have no trouble finding his or her way through the streets of the 'modern' day Venice. The churches and markets are all still in the same place. The Grand Canal ferries still depart from the same stations that they used 500 years ago. Venice manifests continuity like Singapore manifests change. A visitor to Venice will form a deep emotional bond with the city. But a visitor to Singapore will not. Because Singapore is practical, logical and driven. And so it is left to prospective beta humans to reflect and weigh up whether the endeavour to upgrade operating systems is only about an unspoken collective mission to build a better society that elevates all human beings, or whether they must additionally endeavour to build a rich and fulfilling world that is also loaded with social and emotional beauty and nourishment. Because in the rush to embrace the upgrade of its technology and trade, Singapore risks forgetting its more human side. And it is telling that in conversation with Singaporean locals, the most common response when asked what they liked to do with their weekends is to "fly somewhere else".

There is another reason that Singapore cannot yet become the standard bearer for beta humans. And to understand it requires a four-hour flight from Singapore to visit another (former) city-state that was also shaped by British rule and modelled on an unbridled drive toward upgraded modernity and free trade: Hong Kong.

The Union Flag was first raised over Hong Kong in January 1841 when the island had a population of 7,450 fisherman and charcoal burners who lived in its coastal villages. By the time that Great Britain ceded the city-state to China in 1997 the population was 6.5 million. The fact that Britain had to return Hong Kong to China in 1997 is almost an accident of history. The treaty of Nanking ceded Hong Kong to the British in 1832. It was the end of the Opium war and Britain's naval command of the sea left China with little choice. By 1898 food and water were abundant in Kowloon and the New Territories but in very short supply on the barren rock of Hong Kong island across the harbour. The British pledged to give back the New Territories and Kowloon to China and signed a 99-year lease on them to seal the deal. But the British of 1898 didn't think that they would ever have to also give back Hong Kong island too, and so it wasn't included in the deal because, after all, who would ever want the return of that useless and barren rock of nothingness?

In 1984 British Prime Minister Margaret Thatcher contemplated returning Kowloon and the New Territories to China but retaining Hong Kong island, which was not governed by the century-old lease agreement. But the practicality of retaining Hong Kong island in British hands with Kowloon in Chinese hands weighed heavy, and Beijing let it be known that they would march the People's liberation Army into Hong Kong and take it by force if necessary. And so on a rainy night in June 1997, the 260-island rocky Hong Kong archipelago, which had developed into the most dramatic city scape in the world, saw the Union Jack fall and the Chinese flag was raised over the city.

Much like Singapore, Hong Kong holds a special place in my own family history, because having been born in Singapore, it was in Hong Kong that my mother spent her early childhood. I have visited Hong Kong frequently, and every time that I visit my mother always insists that I must do one thing to mark the occasion: to ride the Star Ferry from Hong Kong island to Kowloon on the other side of Victoria Harbour. The Star Ferry has been operating since 1888 and now carries 70,000 passengers a day between Hong Kong Island and Kowloon. The service is primarily operated by very charming ferries from the late 1950's, and so it is entirely possible for me to sit upon the wooden benches upon the deck of one of the white-and-green iron ferries and make the exact journey on the exact same ferry that my mother once rode each day from the British Army base in Kowloon to her school on Hong Kong Island.

The 'modern' ferry service is largely superfluous, since both sides of Victoria Harbour are connected by a world-class infrastructure system of road and rail tunnels. Yet millions of people still climb aboard the charming Star Ferry boats and have a great affection for them, precisely because after more than a century, they are still reliable. And it's not just tourists who use the ferry. Yes it gives the best view of one of the world's most iconic harbour cityscapes; and it has been named by National Geographic as one of fifty things that every traveller "must do" in their lifetime. But the passengers on board are just as likely to be locals who recognise that not all technological progress is indeed 'progress'. Locals could catch the MTR metro system and it will be much faster and cheaper. But there is also a pleasure in riding the Star Ferry – an entirely pointless pleasure in the same way that art and music are pointless pleasures with no real purpose, but are also what make us human.

Each time that I ride the ferry the call with my mother the next day usually goes the same way:

"Did you ride the ferry?"

"Yes mum I did."

"I can remember riding the ferry for twenty minutes every day to get to school and then doing the same every evening."

"It only takes ten minutes now."

"No! They must be using faster boats now then."

"It's literally the same boats as when you were a child Mum."

My mother's confusion is actually valid. In the 1950's the width of Victoria Harbour was 2,300 metres when measuring from Johnson Road in Wan Chai to Chatham Road in Tsim Sha Tsui. Today it has been squeezed to just 910 metres - less than half of its original width – thanks to harbour reclamation to create more land. Such is the extent of the reclamation, that the handsomely colonnaded and domed building of the Old Supreme Court, which once graced the harbour front on one side when it was completed in 1912, now stands more than three hundred meters away from the shore. The Old Supreme Court was itself originally built on reclaimed land that was created by driving hundreds of piles made from Chinese fir trees into the harbour floor.

The reclamation of new land from the sea is a recurring attribute for highly ambitious cities like Dubai, Singapore and Hong Kong. Prior to 1998 passenger jets had to quite literally navigate between the tall buildings of Kowloon to land on the single runway of the over-capacity airport. Local people could look out of their high rise windows and watch landing passenger jets fly past immediately below them. So in 1991 Hong Kong began construction to reclaim 9.38 square kilometres of new land from the sea, and just seven years later, the most expensive airport project in global history opened to great acclaim. It was ranked by the global construction industry as one of the top construction achievements of the twentieth century.

To get a good look at Hong Kong airport you really have to ride the Ngong Ping 360 gondola lift. One of the most enthralling aspects of life in Hong Kong's is that at one moment you can be deep in the heart of its orderly urban jungle, and less than twenty minutes and an inexpensive taxi ride later you can be sitting on the sand on a deserted beach without a care in the world. Most people believe that Hong Kong consists only of skyscrapers and bright neon lights, but it also has long stretches of glorious white sand at over fifty beaches that are a refuge from the city centre, as well as hiking in the New Territories. So if you have any thirst for life you can finish your hectic office job at 5pm and by 5.30pm be watching the sunset from a vibrant beach cocktail bar in Repulse Bay, or enjoying the British-style pub in Stanley, whilst wondering why you would ever want to live your life any other way anywhere else.

Having spent a lot of time in Hong Kong previously, on one of my recent visits I wanted to make more effort to discover the surrounding islands of the New Territories, and so I took a ferry to Lantau Island and found myself sat on the deserted white sands of Cheung Sha Beach. It's not the most beautiful beach in the world, but it is quiet and long enough (3km) to walk bare foot with your feet in the water whilst gazing out to sea and getting lost in thoughts of quiet contentment. The beach is bordered by a forested area that contains a stream and a smattering of houses. There's also a pathway that you can use to walk up stream and through some small villages to observe a fairly modest waterfall, though mostly what you will observe is the occasional tourist looking confused about what it is that they're supposed to be enjoying by walking this trail.

After enjoying the beach for a while I boarded a comfortable and air conditioned public bus toward the Tian Tan Big Buddha on the other side of Lantau Island. The Big Buddha is one of the biggest tourist attractions in Hong Kong. To get to it I had to walk through temple-style buildings that had been converted into a retail village, whilst trying my best to avoid the ubiquitous Chinese tour groups who were all excitedly having their photos taken with the 'sacred' cows that freely wander around the former monastery complex. The cows are so used to the tourists that they are fairly nonchalant about them. Unfortunately getting up close and personal with a cow is such a novelty for many city-dwelling Chinese tourists, that they tend to struggle to contain their excitement, and so occasionally a cows' patience would break and it would headbutt one of the excitable tourists out of the way, much to their surprise. This was terrific entertainment, and had there been a café nearby, I could have quite happily sat and watched this 'man versus beast' phenomenon all day long. But instead I progressed to make the pilgrimage that so many tourists now make, by climbing the 268 steps to the huge bronze statue at the summit.

For me the 'Big Buddha' is another one of those Asian attractions that is built primarily to snare the type of Western tourists who have a penchant for life-affirming 'spiritual' experiences. Admittedly it has been built in a striking position atop Lantau Peak amidst the Po Lin Monastery. But the 34-metre-high bronze statue is entirely modern: it was built between 1990 and 1993. And so to climb its steps is not to tread in the footsteps of many generations of others who have done the same before you in search of spiritual affirmation. It does not give you the feeling of ritual connection across hundreds of years that you get when walking the streets of Pompeii or Venice. It is the epitome of Instagram tourism: you visit because other tourists have done the same very recently before. You take your photo with the giant Buddha. And you post it online. Tick.

The huge statue wasn't the main reason that I had taken the bus onto Lantau Peak. It was also the station for one end of the 5,700 metre long Ngong Ping Cable Car that connects the island with Hong Kong. The epic cable car took its maiden voyage on 18 September 2006 when, in keeping with Feng Shui traditions, just 1,688 tickets were made available at a cost of HK$88 each, because those numbers were considered to be lucky. And it must have worked. Because after paying a little extra to ride in a glass-bottomed cabin, taking the 25-minute journey is a serene and peaceful experience that I enjoyed tremendously. The cable car serves no real purpose. It was built solely as an exposition of modernity that it was thought would also spread some tourist spending onto Lantau Island. And with more than five thousand passengers riding the cable car each day, it represents the kind of economic improvement that is available from basic infrastructure development.

Infrastructure investment comes into focus once more as the cable car passes by Hong Kong airport and you get a full aerial view of the magnitude of the engineering achievement. The airport lies on a completely flat 'platform' on the sea at the foot of a mountainous island. It's elevation is such that it could never be mistaken for not being man made. And to see an entire piece of ocean mastered, conquered and then colonised by a huge modern airport is to observe yet another triumph of modern humanity.

When it comes to mass transport Hong Kong is also far ahead of most Western nations. And in an important lesson for aspiring beta humans, this lead is not always a function of superior technology or even more investment, but is usually a simple function of better operating system design. It is normal for example, to check in your bags for an upcoming flight at a metro station in the centre of Hong Kong many hours before you need to travel to the airport, which is outside the city, thus leaving you free to enjoy the city and reducing the amount of contingency time that you need to allow for being at the airport. And when you do travel on the Hong Kong MTR (metro) it is extremely cheap. This is in part because the operating system of the MTR was deliberately designed to be financially self-perpetuating. The MTR owns a lot of the land above its stations and all of the 'land' within them, and so by developing that land with high density commercial and office space the MTR is able to derive a rental income that subsidises the costs of operating the network. This translates into very cheap journeys for passengers. Of course this does mean that sometimes Hong Kong can feel like one big mall. During the summer months just a few minutes outside in the extreme humidity will make a visitor as wet with perspiration as they would get in torrential rain, so it is advisable to travel around using the network of interconnected walkways that are often linked to the MTR, and as you do, shopping and retail permeates everywhere. But regardless, the notion of building infrastructure that can self-perpetuate and fund itself is another example of lateral thinking at the design stage

311

of big projects that remains too absent in the West. And it offers a key precept for beta humans: that something cannot be considered as 'upgraded' simply by virtue of its being new. An 'upgrade' must mean that by design, something will perpetually confer superior benefits upon all humans very far in excess of whatever operating system has preceded it.

Of course many operating systems in the West already exist, and conventional wisdom is that the opportunity to truly upgrade their operation has long since passed. But socially-vital infrastructure and facilities still need upgrading for every new generation. The world's first underground railway opened in London in 1863 between Paddington and Farringdon. It used gas-lit wooden carriages hauled by steam locomotives. By 1884 there were over 800 trains running on the new 'Underground' every day. Today the London Underground has amalgamated those early privately-funded lines and now includes 249 miles of track - only 45% of which is actually underground - and handles 1.37 billion passenger journeys each year. The London

Tube map which is a classic diagrammatic that was inspired by electrical circuit diagrams and designed by Harry Beck in 1933 for a fee of ten guineas, or about $14 in today's money, is an iconic image.

But few Londoners would claim that using the Underground is a particularly enjoyable experience, because it is barely designed for modern-day city life. A journey on the London Underground will leave you feeling dirty, especially a few hours after your journey when the soot that you have breathed into your lungs finds its way back out of your body as black bogeys. By contrast the first thing that you notice on the Hong Kong MTR is just how clean it is. Nobody leaves litter or discarded newspapers. The metal seats are given an anti-bacterial coating and are regularly disinfected against germs, and the air conditioning provides ice-cool air throughout your journey. The platforms are large and have doors that separate passengers from the approaching trains and, in what is perhaps the biggest sign that Hong Kong has retained many of the 'British' manners that Britain has long forgotten, the etiquette for boarding and disembarking a train is impeccable. Locals form four orderly queues outside each set of doors upon arrows indicated on the floor, leaving plenty of room for disembarking passengers to get past, and then they embark gracefully in formation. There is no pushing or shoving even at peak times, when the MTR deploys extra teams onto the platforms to guide people toward the best place for them to stand and wait.

The Hong Kong MTR remains polite and orderly even though, like London, its passengers originate from many different layers of society. In that respect Hong Kong feels much 'edgier' than somewhere like Singapore. But it is also not so 'edgy' that you feel unsafe. Once when staying in Stone Town on the island of Zanzibar, just off the Eastern coast of central Africa, I got followed by three ominous-looking men into Suicide Alley and the labyrinth of tiny alleys beyond it. It was in the middle of the Muslim call to prayer so the streets had emptied, and it was only by lucky happenstance that I found safety before getting murdered, when by pure luck I found myself standing outside the old merchants house that I was staying in, despite believing myself to be totally lost. That is the kind of 'edgy' that I can quite happily do without!

By contrast, the 'edginess' of Hong Kong manifests itself in a huge gulf of inequality that becomes visibly apparent every Sunday, when tens of thousands of Filipino women who are employed in domestic roles as housekeepers and child carers are given their day off and descend in their droves onto the streets, where they set up mini-camps made from cardboard boxes in which they gather to gossip and eat the lunches that they have brought with them. It is a sight to behold as the hidden economy of domestic service is brought into the daylight by these economic refugees, who invariably send their salaries back home to their families and so have nothing to do on their day off except sit outside.

On the face of it Hong Kong does not offer the kind of lessons for beta humans that can be drawn from Singapore or Dubai or the West Coast of the USA. But Hong Kong does offer a cautionary tale against the belief that the success of relatively small city states in upgrading their operating systems somehow means that it is easily replicable across the world. Nowhere is that more clearly demonstrated than in Hong Kong.

Since China took control, the overtly capitalist former city-state and habitual 'upgrader' has had to adjust to being 'downgraded' to merely a city, albeit one that still has reasonable autonomy due to its classification as a 'special administrative region' of China. Today Hong Kong is a city that is not profiting from its advantageous position between East and West, but which is caught between them, and which epitomises the dichotomy between the Asian-style model for nation-building and the Anglo-Saxon model for building nations and improving societies.

Where this will lead remains to be seen, but there are indicators all around. One can observe this from the viewing deck atop the 484 metre-high International Commerce Centre on the Kowloon side of the harbour. Having bought my ticket and avoided being coerced into having my photo taken in front of a green screen, I ascended what in 2010 was the fourth tallest building in the world, but which by 2018 had been relegated to eleventh. The ICC was developed by the MTR Corporation, Hong Kong's metro operator, and is thus one of the many buildings providing rental income to the MTR (the ICC has 118 floors of premium office space) which subsidises cheap travel. The ICC looks across the harbour toward the second highest building in Hong Kong: the International Finance Centre 2, which stands at 415 metres. And if you look carefully amongst all of the other skyscrapers that are visible across the harbour from the ICC, you'll also see the HSBC building, now a relative minnow at just 180 metres in height. At the time of its completion in 1985 the HSBC building was the most expensive building in the world, costing $668 million. In the run up to the 1997 handover of Hong Kong to China by the British, the islands residents were starting to panic, and HSBC wanted to plant an inconspicuous stake in the future of the territory. Whatever the Communism Party of China brought to Hong Kong, HSBC's new building was designed to show that capitalism would always have a prominent role. It was to be a beacon of reassurance, and marked the pinnacle Hong Kong's evolution from a high-octane pleasure island where it was advisable to get in quick to make some money before getting out, to a place that built the major infrastructure for its future. The striking and idiosyncratic design of the HSBC building was an unequivocal statement that it would still be 'business as usual' after the handover to China.

Yet looking out at Hong Kong from the ICC today it would be easy to miss the HSBC building. It has become dwarfed by newer, larger Chinese-funded skyscrapers, including the 1990-built Bank of China, a bastion of Chinese might, with the sharp corners of its faceted flanks looking like knife edges wilfully slashing away at the good fortune of its HSBC neighbour.

I finished my trip to Hong Kong sitting in my favourite café: the Tsui Wah 'restaurant'. As well as appropriating the English tradition for respectful behaviour and good manners, another good thing that came of out Britain's control over the territory was the appropriation by locals of the English tradition of drinking tea with a splash of milk. Milk tea was absorbed into Cantonese culture, but with milk scarce in the subtropical climate, a shelf-stable substitute was used instead in the form of evaporated and condensed milk. And so in cafes like Tsui Wah, people order dishes that straddle the Chinese-British divide – fluffy egg sandwiches, ham and macaroni in broth, baked chicken tarts – and all served with a smooth, creamy, dairy-sweet milk tea. Milk tea is as ubiquitous in Hong Kong as coffee and it is also a great leveller. In Tsui Wah, newsstand hawkers and real estate tycoons drink it shoulder to shoulder, often accompanied by a Hong Kong-style French toast, which combines thick-sliced white bread with eggs and coconut jam before being deep fried and topped with a heart-attack-inducing amount of butter and sweet condensed milk. It is the kind of comfort food that can quickly become addictive, and as I sat there, aware that I had a flight to catch in a few hours, I felt extra-relaxed because I had already checked in my bags at the local MTR station.

As I sipped my milk tea and contemplated whether I should order another round of Hong Kong-style French toast, I contemplated how both Singapore and Hong Kong occupy strategic and tactical positions as commercial and economic intermediaries between East and West. Singapore shows beta humans that upgrading the operating systems of an entire country works and does indeed create human betterment. The city state could use its position to show what is possible and to export the beta human philosophy throughout the world. But Hong Kong also shows us in extremis that this form of 'city state' has its own limitations.

The story of Hong Kong shows us that even great successes like Singapore can never truly lead a brave and enlightened new world of beta humans. Because by definition, small city-states are a function of, and are contingent upon, their relationships with the wider world and with their biggest neighbours, such as China.

A city state like Singapore offers more lessons for beta humans than perhaps any other nation in the world right now. It's progress in upgrading the operating system of its education system to achieve single-generation social mobility sets a global benchmark. But Hong Kong then shows us just how easily any trailblazing city-state can be cut back down to size by larger geopolitical forces.

Would-be beta humans have a lot to learn from Singapore. But Singapore is unlikely to lead the beta human movement.

LESSONS FOR A BETA FUTURE
(AN EPILOGUE OF TEN IDEAS)

When Winston Churchill predicted that future empires would be "empires of the mind" it is certain that he did not imagine that these "mind empires" would be confined within national borders. And for beta humans to rise they may also have to accept and acknowledge that a 'mind empire' is the only true catalyst for major global change. The Imperial Empire of Great Britain brought vast upgrades that the country has been trading upon ever since - albeit diminishing annually. The USA has been able to transform the world with its vast empire based on economic power, military might and Hollywood entertainment. And China's audacious Belt and Road Initiative is a clear manifestation of China's empire building, which has improved the prospects of hundreds of millions on humans around the world.

It is empires that best manifest change, though this is not a fashionable view, since throughout history the transfer of power from one empire to another has also been the cause of much human destruction.

Yet a beta human empire of the mind could also be an opportunity to halt the swing of this pendulum of geopolitical power transfer. An empire of the mind cannot be built on an impetus to destroy. The dawn of the beta humans requires the world's first empire of the mind to be built on values that can liberate all humans, regardless of country, to fulfil their potential and to leave the planet in a better place for future generations whilst relying technological 'upgrading' to achieve it.

Humans currently exist at a time of great technological progress. A time where data and artificial intelligence and unimaginable processing power are enabling humanity to make better decisions and to avoid mistakes like never before. A time of great life expectations and of abundant leisure and pleasures which, at least in the West, can mostly be accessed and enjoyed without prejudice or discrimination. And thanks to genomics and robotics, human lives may soon also be longer and even more bountiful. Within a single generation humans may be able to claim back more time to spend with their families and friends and to engage in the pursuit of creative and inventive projects that satisfy their very greatest curiosities whilst the world around them provides for their every need.

But despite this great technological promise, and the betterment that all humans could accrue from the universal upgrading of the world's operating systems, the practical reality is that many of the basic amenities of a quality human life are currently diminishing. In the West the percentage of government revenues that are spent on servicing debt is colossal, and represents an ongoing diversion of national wealth away from the poor who need public services, back to the wealthy elite of the world who own the Government bonds. For a family to service the mortgage on a basic family home in the West requires both parents to work, leaving young children in day care which, no matter how good, can never be a substitute for the nurture of a parent. Younger people are delaying starting a family as they face the prospect of never being able to afford to buy a home, whilst trapped in expensive rental apartments. Education is leaving too many behind, infrastructure is not built to last for centuries and, astonishingly for a species that may soon be able to regard itself as 'highly advanced', humanity is yet to attain a sustainable relationship with the planet and is currently presiding over the wanton destruction of huge parts of the global ecosystem that is rapidly pushing more than one million species into extinction.

Humans are thus still very far from becoming 'beta'.

So it falls to would-be beta humans to first shape the current 'old' world to create the right conditions needed to be able usher in the new one. They can do this by synthesising from ten lessons that can be drawn from the experiences and examples of the West Coast USA, UAE, Japan, Russia, China and Singapore:

Lesson 1: The Democratisation Of Democracy

What is the role of democracy in creating the right
conditions for beta humans to rise? Democracy has led
to upgrading and human betterment in the USA, Japan
and Singapore; but equally the UAE, Russia and most
notably China have been able to 'upgrade' without the
constraints of a universally franchised electorate.

Democracy is indeed riddled with imperfections. In
1947 Winston Churchill declared in the House of
Commons that: *"No one pretends that democracy is
perfect or all-wise. Indeed it has been said that
democracy is the worst form of Government except for
all those other forms that have been tried"*. And either
as a cause or consequence, democratic Governments
often find themselves slow to adapt and change in a
way that Governments who are not encumbered by
democracy do not. During the decade that the British
Government spent debating whether to build a new
third runway at Heathrow Airport in London and
weighing up the significant political consequences,

China, with its ability to act unilaterally and without deference to an electorate, built eight brand new airports every single year.

Yet in truth there is no system that has proven itself to be better for consistently improving human lives than liberal democracy. But there also remains a nagging reality that within liberal democracy, the old systems of party-based duopolies have stubbornly persisted whilst the world around them has changing entirely.

The first problem here, as Churchill noted, is not democracy itself, but rather the way that meaningful democratic influence can only be exercised by the electorate through two extremely narrow 'party' channels which are entirely deterministic, since voters cannot choose their choices.

This is exacerbated because many electoral districts are considered to be 'safe seats'. Seats in the House of Representatives in the United States for example have a strong tendency to become 'safe seats', decreasing the number of contested seats in every electoral cycle. The two-party system is therefore geared toward the entrenched status quo, with very little opportunity for reformers to bring change to the dominant political parties, and no opportunity to elect significant change.

So could beta humans retain democracy but upgrade it to better purpose by eliminating the need for political parties? Perhaps yes. And there's two reasons why.

The first reason is that the notion of political parties is diminishing in relevance in a world of global challenges and opportunities. Political parties could become superfluous in an empire of the mind. Free trade, protecting the natural world, creating a sustainable relationship with the planet, food and medical supply chains, human rights – these are just some of the issues that must be dealt with before beta humans can rise, and all of them are global rather than national in their scope.

For example, over half of the world's wild primate species currently face extinction due to deforestation for agriculture and industry, and it is plainly absurd that this should be regarded as a 'national issue' only for the countries where these dwindling populations of primates reside. It is a global problem of great importance to all humans, which transcends national borders and politics, and yet it is a problem that does not feature at all in the party-political-propositions of most nations, where political parties offer their voters very little direct reach into the truly major global issues.

Yet elsewhere in life technology allows humans to express their preferences across hundreds or thousands of individual choices every single day. So why not 'democratise' democracy and allow humans to express their will on the issues that will shape their world without mediation by generic political parties? Why not diminish the role of political parties and instead divert attention to a diverse spectrum of movements and campaigns whose proponents can ask the difficult questions about the challenges facing the world, and then postulate answers for all humans to then vote upon? And then why not apply these results globally?

Humans worldwide could vote to immediately end the extinction of half of the world's primate species. It would be for their civil servants to enact their will much like they deliver the will of the Government of the day.

The second reason is that artificial intelligence could soon start to take care of a good proportion of voting on behalf of all humans. Given access to a populations Internet history, tax returns, credit card bills and bank statements, algorithms could likely predict the political will of most humans with near-complete accuracy.

The current notion of one of two parties being able to accurately capture the will of all of their citizens is as preposterous as the notion that twelve star signs can accurately pigeonhole the personalities of every human; whereas artificial intelligence could capture individual human preferences across a range of 'issues' and reconcile the majority view on each of them. Artificial intelligence may even be able to reconcile the 'tyranny of the majority' in politics by weighing up human-derived choices against an advanced analysis of their impact, and thus AI could even 'overrule' some decisions that are derived from this form of democracy.

Liberal democracy is almost certainly a prerequisite for beta humans to rise. But it probably needs to look very different. Beta humans must 'democratize' democracy.

Lesson 2. Tax Free Ports

Margaret Thatcher advocated tax free ports in her book 'Statecraft' and Singapore, with its colossal GDP per head, has proven the economically transformative power of becoming a tax free port. By allowing manufacturers to import materials to be processed or assembled, and then to re-export those goods without facing any customs duties, economies could re-establish the secondary industrial base that many have blindly shed in recent decades in favour of tertiary services.

But the case for tax free ports also extends beyond economic arguments. For humans to unite in a global collective endeavour to upgrade the operating systems of the world, then that world must also be open for the free flow of trade, innovations and ideas. Beta humans cannot be globally united whilst barriers exist between them, and tax free ports would remove trade barriers.

This system 'upgrade' would be an easy way to spread the benefits of upgrading into those communities that need it most. In Britain for example, the north of the country has never recovered economically from the loss of its status as a global manufacturing hub. By design, this could be the first location for upgrading the country with an assembly of tax free ports, which would more evenly distribute prosperity across Britain by bringing more R&D, training, education and life opportunities to many in those previously forgotten communities. This same logic could be applied in almost every country.

If tax free ports create jobs that would not otherwise have existed, that will also mean that more families will have parents who are able to access skilled employment, more families will live in nicer homes, be able to afford cars and annual holidays. Young people will have more access to opportunities in the areas where they grew up and so families would be able to remain closer together. New 'model villages' based on the original Hampstead Garden Village model could be built in the newly-established tech and manufacturing hubs that would surround every tax free port. And following the Singapore model, businesses could be engaged to design these beautiful new villages for 'regular' working families. The benefits of tax free ports are all too often overlooked in favour of net tax equations. But the example of Singapore has already proven these benefits. Tax free ports manifest the ideals of the free transfer of technologies and ideas that will in turn enable beta humans to upgrade the world.

Lesson 3. Taxing Processes, Not People

If the future is to be different than it cannot be the same. Technology offers beta humans the opportunity to upgrade the world's operating systems in ways that liberate humans from time-based toil and give them more time to engage in family and human endeavours. Singapore has proven the benefits of committing a large percentage of GDP into innovating and upgrading, but the dichotomy hidden within this approach is the gap between the costs of upgrading and the taxes needed to fund it. Technology offers an opportunity to upgrade the global tax regime and to liberate humans from the heavy burden of supporting indebted Governments.

Would-be beta humans must simply be smarter about how taxation works. Humanity is arriving into a future where 1 trillion sensors are connected to the Internet of Things by 5G. This new reality could prove a tipping point in the enablement of artificial intelligence in every aspect of our daily lives, and this will require unprecedented amounts of data to be processed in data centres around the world. Data usage in the era of the beta humans will be multiples that of the world now.

And if technologies such as AI are going to be doing more of our work for humans, making more decisions for humans and even performing jobs, then it could also bear its fair share of the tax burden too. If humans are to be masters and artificial intelligence is to be their servant, then new technologies such as AI should provide for them, and this can be achieved by taxing data centres based on volume of data processed.

Inevitably this taxation would trickle down within pricing to human consumers, but it would fall more heavily on the wealthy, who tend to consume more processed data. A cleaner uses less data than a financial analyst. The driver of a self-driving car will be using a lot more data than the driver of a manual car. And the US-style technology titans who are famously adept at avoiding taxation at present, will also be paying more through taxes on the data centres that power their enterprises.

This approach of taxing processes rather than people can also extend into other endemic processes. A tax on the delivery of parcels would create a level playing field in retail and disincentivise the kind of excessive consumption that is not sustainable for the planet.

The objective overall would be to liberate human beings from the task of funding the continual upgrading of operating systems, by moving the burden away from humans and onto the technologies and processes that will become endemic and omnipresent in a new world.

Lesson 4. Travel Loans For Young People

Every previous revolution has precipitated huge improvements for humanity, and humans now stand on the brink of a transformative technological revolution that will be unlike anything that humankind has experienced before. The First Industrial Revolution used water and steam power to mechanize production. The Second used electric power to create mass production. The Third used electronics and information technology to automate production. Now the 'Fourth Industrial Revolution' will see a fusion of technologies that blur the lines between the physical, digital, and biological spheres. And brave new solutions for upgrading operating systems will inevitably emerge from the nations that are able to harness the indefatigability of youth to synthesise brand new things.

Aspiring beta humans must therefore rethink the way that so many young people are thoughtlessly filtered into the narrow spectrum of experiences offered by colleges and universities. To channel so much money into a single narrow catalyst for individual economic advancement is to ignore a broad and diverse spectrum of alternative ways that those funds could be allocated to individuals to achieve equivalent or better outcomes.

Mirroring student loans, prospective beta humans could advocate for equivalent loans to be made available for young people to travel and gain new experiences in as many countries as possible, before bringing new connections and opportunities back with them in an entirely modern incarnation of the old 'Grand Tour'.

This would also open up a whole new spectrum of opportunities for the kind of self-improvement that powers social mobility. When I left the deprived post-industrial midlands town where I grew up to go and attend university in what then-seemed to be 'far away' in prosperous Sussex, academia barely featured in my calculus. Instead it was the only opportunity available to escape from a place of extremely limited social and economic possibilities to a place that offered greater promise and potential. Attending University was the only way to access the Government loans that made this life change possible for someone who didn't come from a family with money and connections, and I wager that many young people continue to do the same. And like many who attend University, what I learned in the classrooms and lecture theatres was largely anodyne, but the experiences gained outside of the classroom during that same period were formative and invaluable.

And so if humans are to prosper in the emerging landscape of the Fourth Industrial Revolution, then student loans need to be expanded to also be available to those young people who wish to travel. Because by equipping these younger people with access to a diversity of experiences beyond academia, it is their generation who will lead the world in devising the new technologies and founding the businesses that will enable the upgrading of the world's operating systems.

Lesson 5. Huge Investments Into 'Pointless' Art

The last time I visited Pompei it was very early in the morning at the end of a two week working road trip across Italy. I had started in Milan, where a sculpture outside the Italian Stock Exchange of a huge bronze hand showing a middle finger to the world seemed to channel the spirit of capitalism with remarkable honesty; before moving on to Lake Como, Rome, Florence and finally to Naples, where the standard of driving is so uniquely frenetic that it deserves to be given 'World Intangible Heritage' status by UNESCO in the same manner that is afforded to French cuisine.

My visit to Pompeii was to be the culmination of a piecemeal tour of the former Roman Empire which over the preceding months included hiking along Hadrian's Wall in England, taking in the beautiful mosaics at

Chedworth Roman Villa in Gloucestershire, and picnicking atop the Ancient Roman Bath ruins in Nice in France; before being completely astonished by the vast scale of the ruins scattered across Rome, culminating in the magnificent Roman Forum, which is beautiful in size and stature beyond description.

But Pompeii was very different.

Ancient ruins allow visitors to piece together great histories of empires. But those histories tend to focus on kings and emperors and great wars. Pompei is different because it transports a visitor back to a more mundane history of real everyday people with all of their quirks and flaws. And it does it because of how much of the bustling Roman town of Pompei is remarkably well preserved. There are many things at Pompei that allow a visitor to reach back two thousand years. The layout of the streets. The tracks worn into the paved roads by Roman carts. The intact villas and architecture. The ancient graffiti on the walls. The artefacts and, of course, the plaster casts of those who perished when Mount Vesuvius erupted in 79AD.

But what makes Pompeii even more real to experience is the art. It is the art that screams more than anything else across history that "we were here".

The 'Fourth Style' of Roman Art represents a standard that was lost for nearly one thousand years after the fall of Rome. Equivalent European art didn't start to appear again until the early renaissance of the 1400s. Pompei's huge collection of artworks and wall paintings depicts people, dogs, gods and sports. The art is littered with erotic images of sex with huge penises, oversized erections and associated pornographic images that would send most schoolboys into fits of giggles. The art is beautiful but also cheeky. And it sends a message across the millennia not just that "we were here" but that "we were here, we lived full lives, and we had a good time". Art is an enduring expression of the miracle of human life and the remarkable improbabilities of human existence.

341

This single Roman town of Pompeii might seem an unusual basis to suppose that beta humans should therefore make massive investments in art. But from early cave paintings through to the Fourth Style and then to the Renaissance, nothing else connects humanity across the generations in quite the same way. And as the experiences of China and Singapore show, upgrading societies is folly if in the process societies become devoid of their infallible and flawed humanity.

If a society is succeeding it will generate great art and artworks which serve to 'blow the mind' of a viewer and forces them not to submit their internal software into the control of an operating system, but to think, to question everything, to break down ideas and to rebuild one's self all over again. Pointless art breeds new ideas and inspiration about challenging the conventional thinking and wisdom. Pointless art helps to highlight the absurdities of life, to bring what is most important more clearly into focus and to illuminate life's many possibilities. It is through divergent and 'pointless' art that populations learn not to be obedient to authority but to be free to create new things with the kind of imagination that is fledgling within conformist cultures.

Lesson 6. Resetting Humanity's Relationship With The Planet

There is no doubt that climate change is happening. It has been happening for approximately 4.5 billion years. But whether human activity since the industrial revolution started in 1766 is responsible for this change in climate remains uncertain. There are many powerful media organisations that would like to see man made climate change regarded as scientific fact, in particular the BBC in Great Britain which treats man made climate change as dogma. But there are also many bodies who maintain that there is not sufficient cause-and-effect evidence to support scientific fact. But that is not to say that beta humans should be profligate with the planet's resources: quite the opposite in fact.

In 1980 Perrier sold 12 million bottles of water in Britain. By 1990 it was selling 152 million annually. And by 2018 Britain was consuming 7.7 billion single-use plastic water bottles each year. I can remember clearly when 'mineral water' started to appear on British supermarket shelves in the early 1990s. Before then, the only bottled water that I was aware of was Perrier, which was carbonated and sold in a green glass bottle - presumably to the wealthy elite since it was unfathomable to me, and indeed to most people in the Midlands of England at that time, that anyone would pay good money for a bottle of 'posh' water.

As more accessibly-priced brands of "mineral water" started to appear, my mother became an early adopter. I distinctly remember that our fridge would always be stocked with two bottles of her "special mineral water" which my brother and I were banned from touching. Each day our mother would imbibe a small glass of the bottled water so as to take advantage of the alleged restorative qualities of its minerals. In our flat-roofed terraced house in the middle of the UK, mineral water carried high prestige until the fad dissipated and the public wised up to the fact that the mineral content was barely trace. But by then it didn't matter, because bottled water had become an endemic convenience.

Unfortunately this convenience comes at a great cost to the planet. A bottle of Icelandic Mineral Water bought in London happily declares on its packaging that it is carbon neutral and 100% recyclable, but omits to reference the energy cost of producing the packaging, the environmental cost that the packaging will have at the end of its useful life as a bottle, or the presumably enormous environmental and energy costs of shipping a commodity as ubiquitous and plentiful as water across oceans and countries. And that is before the unseen social costs such as the congestion caused by trucks transporting something as entirely superfluous as water.

Presently all of these environmental and social costs are perceived to be mitigated by the singular claim that a bottle of Icelandic water is "carbon neutral". And since carbon dioxide causes global warming and that is the most urgent issue facing humanity, this should therefore be perceived as a good and acceptable mitigation.

Yet it barely crosses anyone's mind that if humanity had a better relationship with the planet, then this water would not be bottled and shipped around the world in the first place, since doing so consumes environmental and natural resources without any gain to humanity. The is a big gulf between having "no carbon footprint" and actually benefitting the planet by being sustainable.

This is indicative of the bigger issue at play: the entire relationship between humanity and the planet's natural resources. Reducing the level of carbon dioxide being produced does not nearly go far enough and offers too easy an excuse for wider inaction. The ultimate litmus test of a successfully 'upgraded' world will be one in which humans live in complete harmony with the planet. Those who achieve it will truly be beta humans.

The human benefits of every product should therefore be weighed against the cost in energy and natural resources throughout its full lifecycle from inception to recycling, and products that consume disproportionate resources relative to their benefits could face 'reparation taxation' in order to disincentivise their production or shipping and to support the restoration and ongoing protection of the natural world and the nature within it. Products that are particularly corrosive to the environment, such as items using forms of Palm Oil that are directly responsible for the destruction of the habitats of the world's dwindling populations of great apes such as chimpanzees, bonobos and gorillas, should face 'reparation taxation' at such a high rate that Palm Oil is no longer an economically feasible product and producers are forced to find alternatives.

This move away from a dogmatic fixation on carbon emissions in favour of genuine sustainability would also support another prerequisite for beta humans to emerge into an enlightened world of the future: that entire species are not be driven to extinction by humans. That the primates in particular – with whom humans share a close ancestor – are facing likely extinction is a great travesty of the current age. The

347

enlightened humanity of the beta humans must recognise the sensitive balance in the ecology of the natural world, and recognise that the health of the natural world is perhaps the greatest indicator as to whether their upgrading of the worlds operating systems is a success. Because this is the only way that beta humans can fulfil the truth of their responsibility to build a better world to pass on to future generations.

Lesson 7. Free Energy

Every great progression of humanity occurs with an even-greater increase in the demand for, and provision of, energy. Every industrial revolution is at its core a leap forward in humanity's ability to generate and then harness more energy. The Fourth Industrial Revolution will have energy demands so huge that they will make modern demands seem quaint and insignificant.

And it falls to prospective beta humans to consider how to turn this inevitable 'energy thirst' into a substantial advantage. It is simply beyond the imagination of current Governments to contemplate something that in

348

the future might be unremarkably self-evident: that energy could be - and should be - free to all humans.

This would not be the first time that Government has assumed responsibility for something on the grounds that it is of national importance and because the free markets would not otherwise provide an adequate supply. It was 1948 before the NHS was founded in Britain and universal healthcare became a public good funded from general taxation. Early roads, canals and railways started as individual enterprises but are today the responsibility of national Governments too. The building of public parks have huge social and human utility, but there is absolutely no private economic imperative to build them, so it falls to Governments.

So why not make energy a 'free' public good too, funded through taxation? There are lots of nations such as the UAE and China and Japan who are embarking on enormous Victorian-style programs of infrastructure. And there are nations and cities such as Singapore who are investing heavily in technological innovations. But by far the most significant and immediate opportunity to upgrade the world's operating systems would be to invest in new power-generation capabilities of such titanic proportions that they can serve many future generations. To build the energy equivalent of Bazelgettes' London sewer system. And then make that energy free to all at the point of use. Forever.

The benefits of free energy would be substantial across a wide variety of levels of economic and social improvement. Fuel poverty would become a thing of the past. The internal combustion engine would be quickly replaced by clean electric cars, making the air cleaner and reinvigorating the transformative personal transport revolution started in 1908 by Henry Ford, which has done more to improve social and actual mobility than any other technology. Brand new technologies that build on the human capacity to access and experience greater life opportunities would be powered by free energy and so more quickly adopted.

Clean and renewable power technologies are also improving at a rapid pace. It is self-evident that making the permanent universal transition to entirely renewable energy sources and planet-friendly energy infrastructure is also a prerequisite for the rise of beta humans.

Lesson 8. Codifying 'Disruptive' Education

Traditional models of education have been disrupted as quality education has become infinitely more accessible and democratised. An enthusiast can access and 'mine' a seemingly endless 'seam' of knowledge on YouTube and consume thousands of lectures by leaders in their fields. A human can learn more in one long night on YouTube than during an entire term spent in a classroom. The algorithms of YouTube present users with relevant knowledge seams to 'mine' and explore any subject in incredible detail and depth. And this revolution offers a key to unlock the latent talent potential that exists within all human beings.

Good education no longer needs to be purchased at great expense: it is now available entirely for free. All that stands in the way of this 'education devolution revolution' powering unprecedented new levels of social mobility is a reluctance to change the existing systems of accreditation that currently hugely favours centrally-planned institutional education. Yet an enlightened society would not allow this unequal status quo to stand in the way of 'upgrading' social mobility.

The opportunity for prospective beta humans is to define how to codify and accredit education, including 'self-education', for the new information era. An individual human of any age now has access to the tools to become educated in a wild spectrum of subjects at any pace that he or she chooses regardless of his or her age, gender or background. An individual can access a bandwidth of subjects and knowledge far beyond what institutional education has ever been able to offer.

The only missing piece of the puzzle is how to recognise the educational achievements of that individual in a devolved system, and to codify those achievements to make them comparable. By doing so prospective beta humans can establish a key tenet: that anyone with the will to learn can access an excellent education online, and that this education will be recognised in a structured and codified way. This system of codified recognition could bring disruption to the way that talent ascends and create social mobility-enabling meritocracy. Because in an upgraded world of beta humans, no human with the will to do more would ever be prevented from achieving their full potential.

Lesson 9. Creating Public Wealth

Shakespeare offered incisive testimony about debt in Hamlet when Polonius warned his son Laertes to "Neither a borrower or a lender be". Unfortunately, successive Governments have not heeded this good advice. At the time of writing, Government debt in Great Britain and in the United States stands at between 80 and 90% of GDP, depending on the information source and the method of calculation. More than 5% of

Government spending in Britain is consumed by the payment of interest on its debt mountain. In the USA, the annual Federal deficit may top $1 trillion in 2020, with interest payments on track to consume more than 13 percent of the entire Federal budget by 2028.

Rather than face the difficult reality that fundamental change and upgrading of their operating systems is needed, successive governments have instead propped up the untenable and unsustainable status quo with persistent borrowing that has left future generations with an insurmountable burden. It will be near-impossible for future generations to remould their nations into a world of beta humans whilst trapped beneath a debt pile consuming their public budgets.

This is contrary to the self-perpetuating and self-funding-by-design principle that is well illustrates by the Hong Kong MTR or the investment of a percentage of annual Government budgets in innovative research and development in the manner of Singapore.

Upgrading the world's operating systems will be an impossible mission if nations are too financially encumbered and 'boxed in' to be able to invest, adapt and change. And what is more, the passing on of a huge and pervasive debt burden to future generations is the antithesis of the beta human endeavour to improve and upgrade the human experience and pass on better life outcomes and a significantly better world to each future generation.

By contrast, there are other nations which are quite literally investing in their future generations. The $1 trillion Sovereign Wealth Fund (SWF) of Norway is equivalent to more than 226% of GDP. Norway is amongst a cohort of nations with substantial SWF's including the UAE (336% of GDP) and Singapore (179% of GDP). The SWF of China represents a more modest 17% of GDP, but that is a reflection of the nation's colossal GDP: China's SWF is valued at $2,038,000,000,000. There are also Anglo-Saxon nations with substantial SWFs, including Australia and

Canada, who have thus proven that a SWF is entirely compatible with Anglo-Saxon forms of capitalism.

Weak political leadership and a failure to face the tough decisions explains much of the missed opportunity. In Britain the Institute for Public Policy Research found that a UK SWF would today be worth more than £500 billion ($650bn) if successive Governments had followed the example of Norway and invested North Sea oil revenues in a British SWF. Instead, successive governments since 1980 spent the funds reducing taxes.

Prospective beta humans must undertake a pivot that bequeaths public wealth to future generations instead of public debt. SWFs can provide future investment income to support government spending without recourse to accruing debts. A strategy for actually achieving this is already mapped out in the excellent book 'The Public Wealth Of Nations', which surmises that in Great Britain and the United States, national and local governments already own a goldmine of assets in the form of real estate or municipal-owned companies, with a value more than twice their current national debt.

'The Public Wealth Of Nations' notes that a 1% increase in investment return on all public assets in the United States would create new investment income equivalent to the total world spending on R&D - or the entire annual GDP of Australia. A 2% increase would create new investment income equivalent to total world spending on basic infrastructure - or the entire GDP of Great Britain. The solution is thus simple: all public commercial assets should be transferred from public departments and local authorities into a national SWF, where they can be better-managed by professional investment managers to improve investment returns.

Only by bequeathing public wealth to future generations will the beta human notion of the continual upgrade of operating systems for the betterment of all humans, become a viable and practical reality.

Lesson 10.Infrastructure' Investment

Another reason to create SWFs is that it would allow for the better deployment of infrastructure investments in the national interest. With tax free ports, free energy and a process-based system of taxation, the need for all types of infrastructure would increase dramatically.

This would be an opportunity for national SWFs to dispose of lacklustre investments and reinvest the capital in big infrastructure projects that better-serve the public interest, whilst also offering superior investments returns. Much like in Dubai or Singapore, this infrastructure could be an exposition in the application of new technologies. But it could also set a new standard for infrastructure-building in nations that have reset their relationship between humanity and the planets resources and environment.

There are two good reasons for this high-technology infrastructure investment. One is pride. The other is economics - although the two are inextricably linked. In the 1960's, the British and French Governments signed an accord to build a supersonic passenger jet, later named 'Concorde'. The jet engine and the jet liner were still relatively new in their application, and the general feeling was that since the world had already been 'shrunk' by a factor of two by the jet liner, and given that man was about to walk on the moon, it stood to reason that supersonic passenger flight should be within the immediate scope of human and national ambition too. One hundred orders were placed for Concorde, but by the first flight in 1969 most orders had dissipated due the rising cost of fuel, improved communications technologies and a public backlash against the noise of sonic booms. The relative value of being able to travel from London to New York in less than three hours (compared to the six-plus hours than it takes today) diminished as history and economics shifted in favour of slower wide body jets that could handle larger volumes of passengers and freight.

Just twenty Concorde's were made and only fourteen ever saw service, but from 1969 to 2003 the Concorde was modern legend. Families would visit airports just to get a glimpse of Concorde as it landed or took off. Children would race around in school playgrounds with their arms stretched out behind their back to represent Concorde's unique wing shape. And after the late Queen Mother mentioned that whenever she heard the plane approaching her home in London she would go out onto the balcony and wave, it became a tradition that every Concorde flying over London would flash their aircraft headlights in salute. Isn't that fabulous?

As a project, Concorde never made a profit. It was also extremely flawed since hard-pressed taxpayers in Britain and France had effectively subsidised the development of an aircraft that became an exclusive mode of travel only available to the rich and famous. But Concorde gave people in Britain and France belief. Belief that the world was moving forward for the better and that their nations were at the forefront. It gave Britons a reason to believe in their 'Jerusalem' just like winning the race to put a man on the moon gave Americans reasons to believe in the mantra of building "the greatest country in the world". And much like the mantle of the space race has today been picked up by private companies, the number of companies now working on re-establishing supersonic passenger flight is too long to list here. Quite simply, sometimes it takes a Government to show that the impossible can be done, before companies can pick up the baton and work out the commercial economics of a wider application. And because Governments can make investment decisions that spread over very long time horizons, a smart Government will keep hold of the intellectual property and in time achieve an investment return too.

Infrastructure is thus the physical manifestation of a collective and unspoken human endeavour to improve and upgrade the world around them. The skyscrapers of Dubai for example give it a stature that far exceeds its GDP and validate a collective mission to build something that can last for many generations.

The second good reason for building new high-technology infrastructure is entirely economic. Faster transportation such as networks of maglev trains would make it easier to spread people and wealth around nations and so lessen the need for families to live in unhealthy high density urban environments. Truly 'smart' roads such as those being trialled in Singapore mean that goods and services could be transported more easily without becoming stuck in congestion. Combined with brand new ports and also 'unseen' technological infrastructure, these investments will not just improve the lives of people now, but will create the capacity that will be needed for future generations too. They will create bandwidth for unlimited new upgrade possibilities for beta humans.

Whether these are indeed the 'right' policies to create the conditions for beta humans remains to be seen. But what is certain is that the world and policymakers need to elevate their thinking beyond the expediency of the status quo and aspire to 'build better' in the future.

AUTHOR'S NOTE

Convention suggest that travel is nourishment for the soul, whilst answering the great questions about the future of nations requires a robust intellectualism. This is not true. Travel allows you to escape the assumptions of your own reality and, much like good art, to question the conventional wisdom of the status quo and break down your ideas and then reconstruct them in inventive new ways.

It is travel that has given me the moments of life that I regard as the most precious. Watching a colony of thousands of giant fruit bats fly out for their evening hunt in Cambodia. Cruising the awesomely beautiful magnificence of Halong Bay in Vietnam. Cycling in Java. Snorkeling the blue coral reefs of Lombok. These life-affirming moments bring a self-evident clarity to an underlying awareness that many of the systems in which we choose to live undermine large portions of our core life force as sentient human beings. And that we can do better.

363

The systems within which we find ourselves are the result of hundreds of years of history and precedent, and it is better to be alive now than at any other time in all of human history. One only has to look at modern life expectancy, or at the abundance of foods available in the average supermarket, which are far beyond what has ever been available to great Kings or Emperors, to know that humanity is doing very well indeed.

But people also have within them a propensity to improve. It does not take genius to be able to observe societies and nations without deference to the subjective bias of the status quo. Travel also enables this break from deference. And the risk when these observations are ignored is not of a great collapse of societies, but rather that some societies will start to stand still whilst the world moves ahead around them.

Humans stand at the precipice not of the next stage in their evolution, but of the *possibility* of attaining the next stage in evolution. Success could greatly improve life outcomes and the entire human experience. Yet too many humans are trapped in the 'standby mode' of a reversion to the perceived safety of incrementalism. Entire nations are seemingly petrified to confront the need for major changes whilst funding their state-of-denial with debt. And all the time the invisible bonds that bind many humans continue to fray.

More than ever the world needs the 'mission statement' of a collective endeavor to become 'beta humans'. It should be a quest to master and accelerate new technologies to improve the human experience and life outcomes and to make the world a better place. A quest to reestablish an unspoken shared mission for the future of humanity that lives in the hearts and minds of all humans. A quest to give people reasons to believe in the great promise and potential of being a part of the next great evolution of humanity, of becoming beta.

Success will come from the example of our culture, our art, our ingenuity and our compassion. It will come from the bravery of stepping back and asking what a successful world really looks like, and then facing the hard decisions that are now needed to adopt a fresh vision. It will come from all humans working together.

And when all humans of the planet are able to come together peacefully in an unspoken collective endeavor, they may truly be able to call themselves: beta humans.

Printed in Great Britain
by Amazon

60860959R00220